Intelligence Arabic

T0323129

Books in the series

Media Persian
Dominic Parviz Brookshaw

Internet Arabic
Mourad Diouri

Security Arabic
Mark Evans

Media Arabic
2nd edition
Elisabeth Kendall

Intelligence Arabic
Julie C. Manning with Elisabeth Kendall

edinburghuniversitypress.com/series/emev

● Essential Middle Eastern Vocabularies ●

Intelligence Arabic

Julie C. Manning
with Elisabeth Kendall

EDINBURGH
University Press

Edinburgh University Press is one of the leading university presses in the UK. We publish academic books and journals in our selected subject areas across the humanities and social sciences, combining cutting-edge scholarship with high editorial and production values to produce academic works of lasting importance. For more information visit our website: edinburghuniversitypress.com

First published 2017
Reprinted 2019

Edinburgh University Press Ltd
The Tun – Holyrood Road, 12 (2f) Jackson's Entry
Edinburgh EH8 8PJ

Typeset in Times New Roman

A CIP record for this book is available from the British Library

ISBN 978 1 4744 0146 3 (paperback)
ISBN 978 1 4744 0147 0 (webready PDF)
ISBN 978 1 4744 0148 7 (epub)

The audio recordings were produced by Phil Hermina, University of Edinburgh.

Published with the support of the University of Edinburgh Scholarly Publishing Initiatives Fund.

CONTENTS

ACKNOWLEDGMENTS

I would like to offer sincere thanks to K. M. Altamimi for his linguistic expertise, to Dr Joseph Pesce, a constant source of inspiration and encouragement, to Jacqueline Manning for her many insightful comments and suggestions, to Dr Elisabeth Kendall for her exceptional contributions, and to Charles Pruett for his boundless support.

Julie C. Manning

"Words – so innocent and powerless as they are, as standing in a dictionary, how potent for good and evil they become in the hands of one who knows how to combine them."

Nathaniel Hawthorne

USER GUIDE

To enhance your ability to recall the vocabulary and to pronounce it correctly, this book is accompanied by audio recordings of the entire contents of each chapter, recorded in both English and Arabic. The audio recordings can be downloaded from our website and are compatible with iPods and other devices.

To access the audio files, please follow the instructions on our website: https://edinburghuniversitypress.com/book-internet-arabic.html

Audio recordings

Main features

- Each Arabic term is recorded with authentic native pronunciation at normal speed.
- Each Arabic term is preceded by its equivalent in English.
- Each chapter is recorded as a single MP3 track (the track numbers correspond to the chapter numbers, e.g. Track 01 = Chapter 1).
- The audio files can be played on a computer or transferred to an MP3 device (e.g. iPod, mobile phone, etc.), enabling you to study on the move.

Tips

- Make sure that you engage actively with the audio recordings by repeating each Arabic term during the pause.
- Pause the recording and challenge yourself to produce the Arabic word before it is announced.

Notes on the formal presentation

This book categorizes intelligence terminology into the following chapters: General, Analysis, Human Intelligence (HUMINT), Operations, Counterintelligence (CI), Signals Intelligence (SIGINT), and Acronyms. While every effort has been made to categorize terms in the most logical way possible, some terms could reasonably be included in two or more categories and judgment calls have been made on their categorization.

The goal of this book is to provide concise, precise definitions for key terms. While some terms have more nuanced meanings in various intelligence agencies, this book seeks to provide the most common, standard definition for each term within the broader intelligence community.

INTRODUCTION

As Western and Middle Eastern states partner to address issues of domestic and transnational terrorism, insurgency and civil unrest in the Middle East and North Africa (MENA), a common understanding of intelligence terms is critical. *Intelligence Arabic* seeks to create a common understanding of key terminology used in English-speaking intelligence communities. Given the often obscure, industry-specific meaning of many of these terms, a glossary of terms alone is insufficient to bridge the linguistic gap between intelligence services. *Intelligence Arabic* offers a concise definition of each intelligence term in both English and Arabic, directly beneath the translation of the term, to facilitate an exact understanding of intelligence community vernacular.

Precision of language and a common understanding of intelligence community terms is key to the success of partnerships between Western and Middle Eastern intelligence services. The distinction, for instance, between "hypothesis" and "assumption" is critical to the intelligence analyst, yet it is commonly conflated in translation. Such miscommunication and the resultant ambiguity of intelligence analysis must not be permitted to impede joint efforts to confront groups and states that threaten the collective security of the MENA region and the international community at large. *Intelligence Arabic* seeks to mitigate the dangers of miscommunication by bridging the linguistic gap between intelligence communities to facilitate clear, precise communication.

1. GENERAL

استخبارات مهمّة تتطلّب ردَ فعل مباشر	actionable intelligence
معلومات استخباراتيّة ذات فائدة مباشرة للمستهلكين	intelligence information that is immediately useful to consumers
استخبارات قائمة على النّشاط	activity based intelligence (ABI)
أنشطة استخباراتيّة مركّزة على أنشطة مجموعة أشخاص مستهدفة أو موقع جغرافيَ	intelligence activities focused on the activities of a target people group or geographical location
تخطيط تكيّفيَ	adaptive planning
قدرة على التّكيّف بسرعة مع الخطط للاستجابة لظروف متغيّرة	ability to adapt plans to rapidly changing circumstances
تهديد مستمرّ ومتقدّم	advanced persistent threat (APT)
عدوَ خطير ومحنّك؛ أو سلسلة من هجمات إلكترونيّة محنّكة وموجّهة	a sophisticated and dangerous adversary; in computer security usage, a series of sophisticated targeted cyber attacks

عدوّ	adversary
شخص أو جماعة أو حكومة أو منظّمة معادية	hostile person, group, government, or organization
منهجيّة التّجميع العدائيّ	adversary collection methodology
أساليب عدوّ في جمع معلومات استخباراتيّة	an adversary's methods of gathering intelligence
الوكالة	the agency
كناية عن وكالة الاستخبارات المركزيّة (CIA) في الولايات المتّحدة	euphemism for the Central Intelligence Agency (CIA) in the US
جميع المصادر الاستخباراتيّة	all-source intelligence
استخبارات مستمدّة من أنظمة استخباراتيّة متعدّدة	intelligence derived from multiple intelligence disciplines
أمان	aman
وكالة الاستخبارات العسكريّة الإسرائيليّة	Israel's military intelligence service
مكافحة الإرهاب	antiterrorism (AT)
تدابير للحدّ من التّعرّض لأهداف إرهابيّة محتملة	measures to limit the vulnerability of potential terrorist targets

تقسيم	apportionment
توزيع موارد محدودة	distribution of limited resources
مصدر معلومات / مصدر موجَّه	asset
مصدر متاح لمنظَّمة استخباراتيّة	resource available to an intelligence organization
مصدر بشريّ	a human source
تهديد غير متناسق	asymmetric threat
قوّة دولة أو مجموعة غير حكوميّة يمكن استخدامها لاستغلال نقاط ضعف عدوّ متفوّق عسكريّاً	a strength of a state or sub-state group that can be used to exploit a militarily-superior adversary's vulnerability
حرب غير متناسقة	asymmetric warfare
حرب بين طرفين ذوي قدرات عسكريّة متباينة بصورة ملحوظة	warfare between two parties with significantly dissimilar military capabilities
ملحق	attaché
مسؤول ملحق بسفارة	official attached to an embassy

قنوات خلفيّة	back channels
شبكات اتّصالات سرّيّة أو غير رسميّة	clandestine or unofficial communications networks
استخبارات أساسيّة	basic intelligence
معلومات أساسيّة عن دولة أجنبيّة أو منطقة أجنبيّة	basic information about a foreign country or area
تجميع ثنائيّ	bilateral collection
نشاطات تجميع منفّذة بالتّنسيق مع جهاز استخبارات أجنبيّ	collection activities carried out in coordination with a foreign intelligence service
قائمة سوداء	black list
قائمة بأسماء الأعداء الّذين يُعتبَر القبض عليهم أولويّة	list of adversaries whose capture is a priority
حدث البجعة السّوداء	black swan event
حدث نادر ولا يمكن التّنبّؤ به وعالي التّأثير	rare, unpredictable, high-impact event

مذكّرة غير معلنة   blind memorandum

مذكّرة مكتوبة دون حاشية   memorandum com-
علويّة للصّفحة أو علامات   posed without
تشير إلى أصلها   letterhead or mark-
ings indicating its
origin

ردّ فعل سلبيّ   blowback

عواقب سلبيّة غير مقصودة   unintended negative
لأنشطة استخباراتيّة تؤثّر   consequences of
على منشئ النّشاط   intelligence activities
which impact the
originator of the
activity

فجوة القدرة   capability gap

إمكانيّة غير كافية لتحقيق   insufficient capability to
الهدف المنشود   achieve a desired goal

حدث كارثيّ   catastrophic event

حادث يسفر عن إصابات   incident resulting in
جماعيّة و/أو دمار   mass casualties
and/or destruction

خليّة   cell

مجموعة سرّيّة صغيرة تشكّل   a small clandestine
جزءاً من شبكة أكبر   group forming part of
a larger network

مركز	center
المقرّ الخاصّ بجهاز استخباراتيّ	headquarters of an intelligence service
مركز الجاذبيّة	center of gravity (COG)
مصدر قوّة يعطي كياناً ما الصّلاحيّة أو الإرادة للتّصرّف	source of strength that gives an entity the power or will to act
رئيس المحطّة	Chief of Station (COS)
رئيس محطّة تابعة لوكالة الاستخبارات المركزيّة	head of a CIA station
CI-21	CI-21
مكافحة التّجسّس في القرن الحادي عشر	counterintelligence for the twenty-first century
استخبارات الطّيران المدنيّ	civil aviation intelligence
استخبارات متعلّقة بتأثير الطّيران العالميّ على الأمن القوميّ	intelligence relating to the impact of global aviation on national security
تحالف	coalition
اتّفاق بين دولتين أو أكثر على العمل المشترك	agreement between two or more states for combined action

collection plan	خطَّة التَّجميع
systematic plan for the employment of resources to collect required information	خطَّة منهجيَّة لتوظيف موارد لجمع معلومات لازمة
collection posture	وضع التَّجميع
the status of an intelligence service's resources to meet intelligence requirements	حالة الموارد المتاحة لجهاز استخباراتيّ لتلبية متطلَّبات استخباراتيَّة
collection requirements	متطلَّبات التَّجميع
information required to answer an intelligence question	معلومات مطلوبة للرَدَ على سؤال استخباراتيّ
common operational picture (COP)	صورة عمليَات مشتركة
display of information shared by multiple commands	عرض معلومات تتشاركها قيادات متعدَّدة
complex catastrophe	نكبة معقَّدة
incident resulting in the failure of critical infrastructure leading to mass casualties or destruction	حادث يؤدِّي إلى إخفاق في البنية التَّحتيَّة الحيويَّة ممَّا يؤدِّي إلى حدوث إصابات جماعيَّة أو دمار

قيد	constraint
متطلّب يحدّ من حرّية التصرّف	a requirement that limits freedom of action
مستهلك	consumer
شخص تعدّ من أجله المنتجات الاستخباراتيّة (أنظر زبون)	a person for whom intelligence products are prepared (*see also* customer)
الولايات المتّحدة القارّيّة (CONUS)	Continental US (CONUS)
أراضي الولايات المتّحدة الأمريكيّة ومياهها القارّيّة	US Territory and its continental waters
حادث طارئ	contingency
حدث مستقبليّ محتمل يتطلّب ردّاً عسكريّاً	potential future event which would require a military response
استمراريّة الحكومة	continuity of government (COG)
جهود لضمان استمراريّة الوظائف الأساسيّة للحكومة في حالة الطوارئ	efforts to ensure the continuation of essential government functions during emergencies

حرب مكافحة العصابات	counterguerrilla warfare
عمليّات ضدّ مقاتلي العصابات	operations against guerrilla fighters
مكافحة الإرهاب	counterterrorism
إجراءات ضدّ المنظّمات الإرهابيّة	actions against terrorist organizations
مركز مكافحة الإرهاب	Counterterrorism Center (CTC)
قسم تابع لوكالة الاستخبارات المركزيّة المكلّف بمهمّة مكافحة الإرهاب	division of the CIA tasked with combatting terrorism
مكافحة التّهديد الماليّ	counterthreat finance (CTF)
جهود مبذولة لمنع تدفّق الأموال إلى الأعداء	efforts to prevent the flow of money to adversaries
مكتب الدّولة	country desk
مكتب تابع للوكالة في بلد أجنبيّ	the agency's office in a foreign country

أبناء العمّ	cousins
عبارة يستخدمها ضبّاط الاستخبارات البريطانيّون والأمريكيّون للإشارة إلى بعضهم البعض	expression used by British and US intelligence officers to refer to one another
عبارة تستخدمها أجهزة الاستخبارات الإسرائيليّة للإشارة إلى العرب	expression used by Israeli intelligence services to refer to Arabs
مصادر معلومات هامّة	critical assets
مصادر معلومات هامّة يؤدّي فقدانها إلى تداعيات سلبيّة للغاية على دولة أو وكالة	important assets whose loss would have extremely negative ramifications on a country or agency
بنية تحتيّة حيويّة	critical infrastructure
بنية تحتيّة يؤدّي تدميرها إلى تهديد الأمن القوميّ أو الاستقرار السّياسيّ أو الاستقرار الاقتصاديّ	infrastructure whose destruction would threaten national security, political stability or economic stability
استخبارات هامّة	critical intelligence
استخبارات حاسمة تتطلّب اهتماماً فوريّاً	crucial intelligence requiring immediate attention

أهميّة	criticality
مصطلح مستخدم لوصف مدى الضّرر الّذي ينشأ عن فقدان البنية التّحتيّة الحيويّة أو تلفها	term used to describe the extent of damage that would arise from loss of or damage to critical infrastructure
تقنيّة هامّة	critical technology
تقنيّة ذات أهميّة حاسمة بالنّسبة لإمكانيّات دولة أو جماعة	technology crucial to the capabilities of a state or group
استخبارات ثقافيّة	cultural intelligence
معلومات حول عوامل ثقافيّة مستخدمة للتّنبّؤ بأنشطة مجموعات من النّاس	information about cultural factors used to anticipate activities of people groups
زبون	customer
دائرة حكوميّة يتمّ تقديم المنتجات الاستخباراتيّة لها (أنظر مستهلك)	government department to which intelligence products are provided (*see also* consumer)
ضرر	damage
انخفاض في الكفاءة ناتج عن أنشطة عدوّ	decreased effectiveness resulting from an adversary's activities

database قاعدة بيانات

information stored for user access معلومات مخزَّنة متاحة للمستخدم

deconfliction تنسيق

sharing information regarding collection activities with other agencies to avoid duplicated or conflicting efforts تبادل معلومات بشأن نشاطات تجميع المعلومات مع وكالات أخرى لتجنّب تعارض الجهود المبذولة أو ازدواجيّتها

defense readiness condition (DEFCON) حالة الجهوزيّة الدَّفاعيّة (DEFCON)

alert levels used by the US Armed Forces; DEFCON 5 is the lowest level of alert, whereas DEFCON 1 is the highest level of alert مستويات تأهّب تستخدمها قوّات الولايات المتّحدة المسلّحة؛ يُعتبَر DEFCON 5 بمثابة أدنى مستوى من التأهّب بينما يُعتبَر DEFCON 1 بمثابة أعلى مستوى من التأهّب

desk مكتب

an agency office dealing with a particular region or topic مكتب تابع لوكالة تتعامل مع منطقة معيّنة أو موضوع معيّن

detainee معتقل

individual captured by an armed force فرد تحتجزه قوّة مسلّحة

ردع deterrence

منع عدوٍ من إجراء فعل ما خشيةً من عواقب ذلك الإجراء preventing an adversary from taking an action through fear of the consequences of that action

مديريّة العلوم والتّكنولوجيا Directorate of Science and Technology (DS&T)

مكتب تابع لوكالة الاستخبارات المركزيّة مسؤول عن البحث العلميَ والتّطوير CIA office responsible for scientific research and development

تنكَّر disguise

إخفاء الهويّة الحقيقيّة لشخص أو شيء ما concealment of the true identity of a person or thing

نشر disseminate

توزيع معلومات ذات صلة (بالقضيّة) على المصرّح لهم بتلقّيها to circulate relevant information to those authorized to receive it

إبعاد distancing

فصل شخص أو منظّمة خاصّة بشخص عن شخص آخر أو منظّمة أخرى separating oneself or one's organization from another individual or organization

استخبارات محلّيّة	domestic intelligence
استخبارات متعلّقة بأنشطة داخل وطن جهاز استخبارات معيّن	intelligence regarding activities within a service's home country
إرهاب محلّيّ	domestic terrorism
إرهاب يرتكبه مواطنو الدّولة المستهدفة	terrorism perpetrated by nationals of the target country
استخدام مزدوج	dual-use
أشياء يمكن استخدامها لأغراض مدنيّة وكذلك لأغراض عسكريّة ودفاعيّة	objects that can be used for civilian purposes as well as for military and defense purposes
استخبارات اقتصاديّة	economic intelligence
استخبارات بشأن النّظام الاقتصاديّ لبلد ما	intelligence regarding the economic system of a country
حرب اقتصاديّة	economic warfare
جهود مبذولة لإضعاف دولة بواسطة وسائل اقتصاديّة	efforts to weaken a state through economic means
حالة الانتهاء النّاجح	end state
شروط يجب تلبّيتها لتحقيق هدف محدّد	conditions which must be met to achieve a specified objective

enemy combatant (EC)	مقاتل عدوّ
individual engaged in armed conflict against a state	فرد مشارك في صراع مسلّح ضدّ دولة
essential elements of information (EEI)	عناصر المعلومات الأساسيّة
information critical to timely decision-making	معلومات ذات أهميّة لاتّخاذ القرارات في الوقت المناسب
espionage	تجسّس
clandestine gathering of information	جمع المعلومات سرّاً
evidence	دليل
anything used to determine the truth of a claim	أيّ شيء مستخدم لتحديد صحّة ادّعاء
expeditionary intelligence	استخبارات استكشافيّة
foreign intelligence supporting an armed force	استخبارات أجنبيّة مساندة لقوّة مسلّحة
finding	استنتاج
presidential authorization for a covert operation	تفويض رئاسيّ لعمليّة سرّيّة

الشَّركة	the firm
الاسم الكنية للاستخبارات السَّرِّيَّة البريطانيَّة	nickname for the British Secret Intelligence Service (SIS)
خمس عيون	Five Eyes (FVEY)
أستراليا وكندا ونيوزيلندا والمملكة المتَّحدة والولايات المتَّحدة	Australia, Canada, New Zealand, the United Kingdom, and the US
مضاعف قوَّة	force multiplier
قدرات تزيد من إمكانيّات قوَّة مسلَّحة	capabilities which increase the potential of an armed force
استخبارات أجنبيّة	foreign intelligence
معلومات بشأن أهداف أجنبيّة	information regarding foreign targets
مصلحة أجنبيّة	foreign interest
شخص أو حكومة أو شركة أو كيان أجانبيّ آخر	foreign person, government, corporation, or other entity
أربع عيون	Four Eyes (ACGU)
أستراليا وكندا والمملكة المتَّحدة والولايات المتَّحدة	Australia, Canada, the United Kingdom and the US

عصابة	guerrilla group
مجموعة غير حكوميّة مشاركة في حرب غير نظاميّة	non-state group engaged in irregular warfare
حرب عصابات	guerrilla warfare
حرب غير نظاميّة تخوضها جهات غير حكوميّة ضدّ حكومة	irregular warfare fought by sub-state actors against a government
هدف عالي القيمة	high-value target (HVT)
هدف قد يقلّل فقدانه من قدرات عدوّ	a target whose loss would degrade an adversary's capabilities
إرهابيّ محليّ	homegrown terrorist
فرد مشارك في أنشطة إرهابيّة موجّهة ضدّ وطنه أو الدولة الّتي يقيم فيها	individual engaged in terrorist activities directed against his/her country of citizenship or residency
بلد مضيف	host country
دولة تسمح لكيان أجنبيّ بالعمل داخل حدودها	country which allows a foreign entity to operate within its borders

معادٍ	hostile
وصف عضو مجموعة معادية تمّ تحديدها كمصدر تهديد	description of a member of an adversarial group identified as a threat
بيئة معادية	hostile environment
منطقة تخضع لسيطرة قوَات معادية	area controlled by adversarial forces
نوايا معادية	hostile intent
تهديد وشيك بهجوم مسلّح	imminent threat of an armed attack
تجسّس صناعيّ	industrial espionage
تجسّس ترتكبه شركات لأغراض تجاريّة	espionage perpetrated by corporations for commercial purposes
معلومات	information
بيانات والمعاني المخصّصة للبيانات	data and the meaning assigned to the data
تمرّد	insurgency
ثورة مسلّحة ضدّ حكومة	armed rebellion against a government

استخبارات	intelligence
معلومات لتلبية احتياجات مستهلكين	information to meet the needs of consumers
عمليّة تحديد وجمع وتحليل وتعميم المعلومات	process of identifying, collecting, analyzing, and disseminating information
أجهزة تتعامل في مجال تجميع وتحليل المعلومات الاستخباراتيّة	organizations which deal in intelligence collection and analysis
تجميع استخباراتيّ	intelligence collection
حصول على معلومات استخباراتيّة	obtaining intelligence information
مجتمع استخباراتيّ	intelligence community (IC)
مجموعة من أجهزة استخباراتيّة تعمل بشكل مستقلّ وكذلك سويّاً	group of intelligence organizations that work both independently and together
ضابط استخباراتيّ	intelligence officer
فرد موظّف من قبل جهاز استخباراتيّ	individual employed by an intelligence service

رقابة على الاستخبارات	intelligence oversight
مراجعة مستقلّة لجهاز استخباراتيّ لضمان الامتثال لقوانين معمول بها	independent review of an intelligence service to ensure compliance with applicable laws
عمليّة استخباراتيّة	intelligence process
عمليّة تخطيط وجمع ومعالجة وتحليل وتعميم معلومات استخباراتيّة	process of planning, collecting, processing, analyzing, and disseminating intelligence information
تقرير استخباراتيّ	intelligence report (INTREP)
تقرير عن وضع يتطلّب توزيع سريع	a report about a situation which requires rapid dissemination
متطلّبات استخباراتيّة	intelligence requirements
حاجات محدّدة لاستخبارات حول موضوع معيّن	identified needs for intelligence on a given topic

intelligence source مصدر استخباراتيّ

individual, group, system or other means used to collect information فرد أو مجموعة أو نظام أو وسائل أخرى مستخدمة لجمع المعلومات

intelligence summary (INTSUM) ملخّص استخبارات

summary of intelligence information covering a designated period of time ملخّص معلومات استخباراتيّة يغطّي فترة محدّدة من الوقت

intelligence, surveillance and reconnaissance (ISR) استخبارات ومراقبة واستطلاع

synchronization of the collection and processing of information about a target مزامنة تجميع معلومات حول هدف ما ومعالجتها

interagency coordination تنسيق بين وكالات

coordination between domestic and/or international agencies تنسيق بين وكالات محليّة و/أو دوليّة

دفاع داخليّ	internal defense
جهود حكومة لحماية بلادها من عناصر تخريبيّة	a government's efforts to protect its country from subversive elements
أمن داخليّ	internal security
جهود لمنع أعمال معادية وللحفاظ على السّلام داخل حدود بلد	efforts to prevent hostile acts and to maintain peace within a country's borders
إرهاب دوليّ	international terrorism
إرهاب يستهدف بلداً أجنبياً أو يعبر حدوداً دوليّة	terrorism aimed at a foreign country or that crosses international boundaries
قوّات غير نظاميّة	irregular forces
جهات مسلّحة غير حكوميّة	armed sub-state actors
حرب غير نظاميّة	irregular warfare
صراع مسلّح بين جهات حكوميّة وغير حكوميّة	armed conflict between state and non-state actors
مساعد رئيسيّ	key enabler
عنصر حاسم لازم لتلبية هدف	crucial element required to meet an objective

جهاز اتّصال	liaison service
جهاز أجنبيّ يتعاون معه جهاز معيّن	foreign service with which a service cooperates
ميمونيه	Memuneh
لقب في إسرائيل لرئيس الموساد	in Israel, title for the head of Mossad
MI5	MI5
جهاز الأمن الدّاخليّ البريطانيّ	British internal security service
MI6	MI6
الجهاز البريطانيّ للاستخبارات الخارجيّة	British foreign intelligence service
مهمّة	mission
مهمّة موكّلة أو واجب موكّل لفرد أو وحدة	task or duty assigned to an individual or unit
أسلوب عمل	modus operandi (MO)
مميّزات طريقة عمل فرد أو منظّمة	an individual's or organization's characteristic method of operating

مراقبة ومنع	monitoring and preventing
استخبارات تهدف إلى منع ومراقبة أنشطة إجراميّة	intelligence aimed at preventing and monitoring criminal activities
موساد	Mossad
الجهاز الإسرائيليّ للاستخبارات الخارجيّة	Israeli foreign intelligence service
إرهاب (مموّل عبر) تجارة المخدّرات وتهريبها	narco-terrorism
إرهاب مرتبط بتجارة المخدّرات	terrorism linked to drug trafficking
الجهاز السّرّيّ الوطنيّ	national clandestine service (NCS)
جهاز استخبارات تابع للولايات المتّحدة مكلّف بعمليّات سرّيّة	US intelligence service tasked with clandestine operations
المركز الوطنيّ لمكافحة الإرهاب	National Counterterrorism Center (NCTC)
منظّمة أمريكيّة مهمّتها تكامل وتحليل معلومات استخباراتيّة متعلّقة بالإرهاب	US organization tasked with integrating and analyzing intelligence relating to terrorism

تقدير الاستخبارات الوطنيّة	National Intelligence Estimate (NIE)
في الولايات المتّحدة، تقرير يجمل إجماع آراء شتّى عناصر المجتمع الاستخباراتيّ حول موقف موضع الاهتمام	in the US, a report outlining the consensus of the various elements of the intelligence community on a situation of interest
ضوضاء	noise
ورود معلومات لا قيمة لها بالموضوع مع معلومات ذات قيمة	irrelevant information received along with valuable information
منظّمة غير حكوميّة	non-governmental organization (NGO)
منظّمة خاصّة غير ربحيّة	a non-profit, private organization
ضابط	officer
فرد موظّف لدى وكالة الاستخبارات لجمع و/أو تحليل معلومات لتلك الوكالة	individual employed by an intelligence service to collect and/or analyze information for that service
مصدر مفتوح	open source
متاح للعموم	publicly available

ترتيب معركة	order of battle (OB)
معلومات بشأن هيكليّة وإمكانيّات قوّة عسكريّة	information regarding the structure and capability of a military force
علنيّ	overt
أنشطة تتمّ علناً	activities done openly
قوّات شبه عسكريّة	paramilitary forces
وحدات من جنود ليسوا جزءاً من القوّات المسلّحة الرّسميّة للدّولة	units of soldiers who are not part of the formal armed forces of the state
أمن جسديّ	physical security
أمن الموظّفين والمرافق والوثائق والمعدّات	security of personnel, facilities, documents, and equipment
دوائر متكاملة	piggybacking
استخدام معلومات استخباراتيّة يجمعها ويتشاركها جهاز استخباراتيّ أجنبيّ صديق	using intelligence collected and shared by a friendly foreign intelligence service

نكران يمكن تصديقه	plausible deniability
مقدرة فرد أو حكومة على نفي أيّة مسؤوليّة عن حدث ووجود مصدر بديل ذي مصداقيّة لهذا الحدث	ability of an individual or government to deny any responsibility for an event and the existence of a credible alternative source of the event
تنميط	profiling
تقييم التّهديد الّذي قد يشكّله فرد ما على أساس عوامل معروفة عنه (مثل عرق أو دين، إلخ)	assessing the threat an individual may pose based on known factors (such as race, religion, etc.)
انتشار	proliferation
بيع أو نقل أسلحة الدّمار الشّامل إلى جهات معادية	sale or transfer of weapons of mass destruction to hostile actors
الوقت الفوريّ	real time
الوقت الفعليّ الّذي يجري فيه حدث ما	actual time in which an event occurs
معالجة	remediation
إجراءات لتصحيح نقاط ضعف محدّدة	actions to correct identified weaknesses

تسليم استثنائيّ	rendition
قبض على فرد في بلد أجنبيّ دون موافقة ذلك البلد ونقله إلى بلد آخر	apprehending an individual in a foreign country without that country's approval and moving him/her to another country
إعادة إلى الوطن	repatriation
إعادة أفراد إلى موطنهم الأصليّ	returning individuals to their home country
مخاطرة	risk
عواقب سلبيّة محتملة مرتبطة بتهديد	potential negative consequences linked to a threat
تطهير	sanitization
إزالة أسماء و/أو تفاصيل رئيسيّة من تقرير	to remove names and/or key details from a report
مصادرة	seizure
حجز مصرّح به على فرد أو ممتلكات	authorized seizing of an individual or property
وعي ظرفيّ	situational awareness
وعي بالظّروف المحيطة بفرد أو عمليّة في أيّ وقت محدّد	awareness of the conditions surrounding an individual or operation at any given time

إبلاغ مباشر	stovepiping
نقل معلومات مباشرةً إلى قمّة التّسلسل الهرميّ	transmitting information directly to the top of a hierarchy
استخبارات استراتيجيّة	strategic intelligence
استخبارات لازمة لتخطيط سياسة واستراتيجيّة وعمليّات عسكريّة	intelligence required for planning policy, strategy and military operations
إرهاب	terrorism
عنف ذو دوافع سياسيّة أو التّهديد بالعنف ضدّ غير المقاتلين	politically motivated violence or the threat of violence against non-combatants
تهديد ماليّ	threat finance
أموال غير مشروعة لتمويل أنشطة غير مشروعة	illicit funds to finance illicit activities
تعرّض للهجوم	vulnerability
ضعف؛ قابليّة التّعرض لتهديد	weakness; susceptibility to a threat

2. ANALYSIS

خطف	abduction
عمليّة إنتاج فرضيّة جديدة لتفسير دليل لا يشير إلى تفسير شائع	process of generating a new hypothesis to explain evidence that does not point to a common explanation
تحليل كافّة المصادر الاستخباراتيّة المتوافرة	all-source analysis
تحليل مبني على معلومات محصّلة من جميع المصادر الاستخباراتيّة المتاحة (الاستخبارات البشريّة واستخبارات الإشارات، إلخ)	analysis based on information obtained from all available sources of intelligence (HUMINT, SIGINT, etc.)
تحليل بديل	alternative analysis
تقنيّة تحليل تهدف إلى تحدّي افتراضات أو تقييمات	analysis technique aimed at challenging assumptions or assessments
تحليل	analysis
عمليّة فحص وتقييم وتكامل بيانات لاستخلاص استنتاجات	process of examining, evaluating and integrating data to derive conclusions
تحليل وإنتاج	analysis and production

عمليّة تحويل معلومات تمّ معالجتها إلى منتجات استخباراتيّة	the process of convert-ing processed information into intel-ligence products
تحليل فرضيّات متنافسة	analysis of competing hypotheses (ACH)
تقنيّة تحليل تهدف إلى القضاء على فرضيّات غير محتملة	analysis technique aimed at eliminating unlikely hypotheses
محلّل	analyst
فرد موظّف لدى وكالة استخبارات لتحليل معلومات	individual employed by an intelligence agency to analyze information
تواصل تحليليّ	analytic outreach
اشتراك محلّل مع أفراد خارج المجتمع الاستخباراتيّ للحصول على رؤى ووجهات نظر بديلة	analyst engagement with individuals outside of the intelli-gence community to gain insights and alt-ernative perspectives
حرفيّة تحليليّة	analytic tradecraft
منهجيّات وتقنيّات مستخدمة في تحليل معلومات استخباراتيّة	methodologies and techniques used in in-telligence analysis
إرساء	anchoring

ميل للاعتماد بشكل أكثر ممّا
ينبغي على معلومة واحدة

bias of relying too heav-
ily on a single piece
of information

حالات شاذّة

anomalies

انحرافات غير عادية عمّا هو
متوقّع

unusual deviations from
what is expected

تقييم

assessment

تقييم مصداقيّة ودقّة و/أو فائدة
مصدر أو نظام استخباراتيّ

evaluation of the credi-
bility, accuracy
and/or utility of intel-
ligence sources or
activities

افتراض

assumption

معلومات صحّتها مفترضة في
عدم وجود دليل

information assumed to
be true in the absence
of proof

توافر

availability

تحيّز في المبالغة في تقدير
احتمال أو تكرار حدث بناءً
على كيفيّة وجود أحداث
سابقة مماثلة ومشهودة في
عقل فرد ما

bias of overestimating
the probability or fre-
quency of an event
based on how memo-
rable previous similar
events are in an indi-
vidual's mind

تحيّز	bias
ميل متأصّل نحو خيار معيّن أو تفسير معيّن مقارنة بآخر	ingrained inclination toward one choice or explanation over another
صورة كبيرة	big picture
نظرة واسعة متكاملة تشمل جميع جوانب القضيّة	integrated, broad view incorporating all aspects of an issue
المهمَ في المقدَمة	bottom line up front (BLUF)
استنتاج تحليليّ موصوف في بداية منتج استخباراتيّ	analytic conclusion delineated at the beginning of an intelligence product
قاعدة إيجاز	brevity rule
قاعدة توجّه محلّلين لاستخدام لغة موجزة ودقيقة في المنتجات الاستخباراتيّة	rule directing analysts to use brief, concise language in intelligence products
تجمّع	clustering
رصد أنماط ليس لها وجود في الواقع	observing patterns where none exist in reality

تماسك	cohesiveness
وصف لتحليل يُعتبَر متكاملاً بشكل جيّد وموحَّداً لدعم استنتاج	description of analysis which is well integrated and unified in support of a conclusion
جمع	collate
مقارنة معلومات متعدّدة متعلّقة بنفس الموضوع	to compare multiple pieces of information regarding the same topic
مستوى الثِّقة	confidence level
مستوى يقين محلّل فيما يتعلّق بدقّة أو مصداقيّة استنتاج أو تقدير	degree of certainty of an analyst regarding the accuracy or credibility of a conclusion or judgment
تحيّز للتّأكيد	confirmation bias
تحيّز للبحث عن أو قبول معلومات لدعم فكرة مسبقة مع تجاهل البيانات الّتي تتعارض مع تلك الفكرة المسبقة	bias of seeking or accepting information to support a preconceived idea while ignoring data that conflicts with that preconceived idea

سياق	context
ظروف محيطة بمعلومات أو بحدث تفيد عن معنى المعلومات أو الحدث	circumstances surrounding information or an event which inform the meaning of the information or event
أفكار أساسيّة	core ideas
مفاهيم رئيسيّة	key concepts
تأييد	corroboration
تحقّق من موثوقيّة معلومات من خلال الحصول على معلومات من مصادر مستقلّة تدعم المعلومات الأوّليّة	verifying the reliability of information through the acquisition of information from independent sources to support the initial information
معلومات ذات مصداقيّة	credible information
معلومات تمّ تقييمها على أنّها معقولة	information assessed to be plausible
تقييم مصداقيّة	credibility assessment
تقييم لتحديد صحّة معلومات	assessment to determine the veracity of information

criteria معايير

metrics used to judge مقاييس مستخدمة للحكم على
   the quality of intelli- نوعيّة التّحليل الاستخباراتيّ
   gence analysis

critical thinking تفكير ناقد

clear, intellectually dis- تفكير بطريقة واضحة منضبطة
   ciplined thinking عقليّاً مبني على سبب وأدلّة
   based on reason and
   evidence

cultural bias تحيّز ثقافيّ

bias of favoring infor- تحيّز لصالح معلومات أو
   mation or conclusions استنتاجات تتّفق مع وجهة
   that are consistent نظر ثقافيّة لمحلّل
   with an analyst's cul-
   tural viewpoint

deduction اقتطاع

a process of reasoning عمليّة استدلال يتمّ فيها
   in which specific con- استخلاص استنتاجات
   clusions are drawn محدّدة من قواعد عامّة
   from general rules (على النّقيض من استقراء)
   (*contrast with* induc-
   tion)

devil's advocacy دفاع الشّيطان

building the strongest بناء أقوى حجّة ممكنة للطّعن
   possible argument to بموقف مقبول على نطاق
   challenge a widely واسع
   accepted position

استخبارات تقديريّة	estimative intelligence
تحليل قدرات عدوّ	analysis of an adversary's capabilities
لغة تقديريّة	estimative language
لغة يستخدمها محلّل لوصف مستوى احتمال و/أو ثقة متعلّقة باستنتاج أو تقدير	language used to describe the level of probability and/or confidence an analyst attaches to a conclusion or judgment
تقييم	evaluation
تقييم مصداقيّة ودقّة و/أو فائدة المعلومات	appraisal of the credibility, accuracy and/or utility of information
تقييم وتعليقات	evaluation and feedback
تقييم مستمرّ لعمليّات استخباراتيّة للتّأكّد من أنّها تلبّي احتياجات الزّبون	continuous assessment of intelligence operations to ensure that they meet the needs of the customer
استخبارات نهائيّة	finished intelligence
منتج جاهز للتّوزيع على زبائن بعد اجتياز دورة الاستخبارات	product that is ready for distribution to customers after going through the intelligence cycle

أدوات الاستفهام الخمس	five w's
من وماذا ومتى وأين ولماذا؛ أدوات استفهام مستخدمة لضمان إعداد تقارير شاملة عن حدث أو موقف	who, what, when, where, why; used to ensure comprehensive reporting on an event or situation
انصهار	fusion
تقييم جميع المصادر المتاحة للاستخبارات لإنتاج تقييم شامل	evaluation of all available sources of intelligence to produce a comprehensive assessment
تفكير جماعيّ	group think
ممارسة مغلوطة في صنع القرار حيث لا تشجّع الرّغبة في المطابقة مع مجموعة على المسؤوليّة الفرديّة وإيجاد الحلول للمشاكل	flawed decision-making practice whereby the desire for conformity with a group discourages individual responsibility and problem solving
استدلالات	heuristics
اختصارات عقليّة يستخدمها العقل بشكل حدسيّ لمعالجة معلومات	mental shortcuts the brain intuitively uses to process information

تحيّز للإدراك المتأخّر	hindsight bias
تحيّز لاعتبار حدث سابق كما لو كان في قدرة الإنسان التّنبّؤ به حتّى وإن لم يكن في قدرته التّنبّؤ به	bias of viewing a past event as having been predictable even when the event may not have been pre-dictable
فرضيّة	hypothesis
تفسير معقول لنظريّة لم تُثبَت حتّى الآن	plausible explanation which has not yet been proven
مؤشّرات وتحذير	indications and warning (I&W)
أنشطة استخباراتيّة تهدف إلى الكشف عن نوايا معادية قبل أن يتمّ تنفيذها	intelligence activities aimed at detecting hostile intentions before they are acted upon
مؤشّرات	indicators
معلومات تشير إلى استنتاج ولكنّها لا تثبّته	pieces of information that point to, but do not prove, a conclu-sion

استقراء	induction
عمليّة استدلال يتمّ فيها استخلاص استنتاجات عامّة من ملاحظات أو أدلّة محدّدة (*على النَّقيض من* اقتطاع)	process of reasoning in which general conclusions are drawn from specific observations or evidence (*contrast with* deduction)
معلومات	information
بيانات أوَليّة يتمّ معالجتها وتحليلها لتوليد معلومات استخباراتيّة	raw data which is analyzed and processed to generate intelligence
فجوة معلومات	information gap
معلومات مطلوبة وغير متوفّرة	required information which is not available
دورة استخباراتيّة	intelligence cycle
عمليّة تحويل بيانات أوَليّة إلى منتج مخابراتيّ جاهز	process of converting raw data into a finished intelligence product
تقييم استخباراتيّ	intelligence estimate
تقييم وضع بناءً على معلومات استخباراتيّة متاحة	assessment of a situation based on available intelligence

فجوة استخباراتيّة	intelligence gap
معلومات مطلوبة وغير متوفّرة	required information which is not available
منتج استخباراتيّ	intelligence product
تقرير استخباراتيّ أعدّه محلّلون وتمّ تقديمه إلى زبون	intelligence report compiled by analysts and provided to a customer
ترجمة	interpretation
تقييم معلومة فيما يتعلّق بجميع المعلومات الأخرى المعروفة عن موضوع معيّن	assessing a piece of information in relation to all other known information about a given topic
متطلّبات استخبارات رئيسيّة	key intelligence requirements
استخبارات ذات أولويّة عالية مطلوبة من قبل صنّاع القرار	high-priority intelligence required by decision-makers
رابط	link
علاقة بين كيانين	relationship between two entities

تحليل مترابط	link analysis
تـحليل العلاقات بين كيانات (*أنظر تحليل شبكة*)	analysis of the relationships between entities (*see also* network analysis)
قالب	matrix
شكل رسوميَ لبيانات مستخدم لإظهار علاقات بين اثنين أو أكثر من مجموعات البيانات	graphic representation of data used to show relationships between two or more sets of data
عقليَة	mindset
معتقدات وافتراضات ومواقف يحتفظ بها فرد وتبيّن أسلوبه في معالجة المعلومات	beliefs, assumptions and attitudes held by an individual which inform the way he or she processes information
انعكاس التّصوير	mirror imaging
فرضيّة أنَّ آخرين يفكّرون ويتصرّفون بطريقة شخص معيّن	assumption that other people think and act the same way a given person thinks and acts

تصوّر خاطئ	misperception
صورة غير دقيقة أو غير مكتملة للواقع؛ فهم خاطئ لشيء معيّن	an inaccurate or incomplete picture of reality; a faulty understanding of something
تحيّز سرديّ	narrative bias
تحيّز إلى تصفية معلومات لا تتناسب مع سرديّة أو إلى إيجاد معلومات لإكمال سرديّة غير كاملة	bias of filtering out information that does not fit with an established storyline or of creating information to complete an incomplete storyline
تحليل شبكة	network analysis
تحليل علاقات بين كيانات (أنظر تحليل مترابط)	analysis of relationships between entities (*see also* link analysis)
وهميّ	notional
خياليّ؛ غير صحيح	fictitious; not true
موضوعيّة	objectivity
تقدير لا تؤثّر عليه العاطفة أو التّحيّز؛ تقدير يستند على أدلّة فقط	judgment free from the influence of emotion and bias; judgment based solely on evidence

رأي   opinion

وجهة نظر أو معتقد لا يستند   a view or belief which
على حقائق ملموسة   is not based on con-
     crete facts

تحليل نمط   pattern analysis

تحليل نقاط بيانات متعدّدة   analysis of multiple
لتحديد أنماط   data points to identify
     patterns

تنبّؤ   prediction

توقّعات محلّل بوقوع أو عدم   analyst's forecast that
وقوع حدث أو موقف معيّن   an event or situation
     will or will not occur

احتماليّة   probability

إمكانيّة وقوع حدث وفقاً لتقييم   likelihood, as assessed
محلّل   by an analyst, that an
     event will occur

تحيّز عشوائيّ   randomness bias

تحيّز لتفضيل تفسيرات منهجيّة   bias of preferring sys-
حتّى إذا كانت الأحداث   tematic explanations
عشوائيّة في الواقع   even when events are
     in fact random

علاقات   relationships

صلات بين كيانات   connections between
     entities

علاقة صلة	relevance
مستوى فائدة معلومات في الإجابة على سؤال استخباراتيّ	degree to which information is useful in answering an intelligence question
إعادة تتبّع التّحليل	retracing the analysis
عمليّة مستخدمة لتحديد كيفيّة حدوث تقييم خاطئ	process used to determine how an incorrect assessment was made
تزييف بأثر رجعيّ	retrospective falsification
تجميل وتحوير قصّة ذات أساس واقعيّ إلى حدّ ما مع مرور الوقت	embellishment and falsification over time of a story with some factual basis
تقييم مخاطرة	risk assessment
تحديد مخاطر وتقييمها	identification and evaluation of risks
منهج علميّ	scientific method
عمليّة استدلال تجمع بين استدلال استقرائيّ واستنتاجيّ	process of reasoning which combines inductive and deductive reasoning

تحليل استراتيجيّ	strategic analysis
تحليل المستقبل مع التَّركيز على اتّجاهات طويلة المدى	analysis of the future, focusing on long-term trends
تركيب	synthesis
ضمّ معلومات استخباراتيّة إلى غيرها من المعلومات الاستخباراتيّة المتوفّرة للوصول إلى نتيجة	combining intelligence information with other available intelligence information to reach a conclusion
تحليل تهديد	threat analysis
تحليل احتماليّة وتأثير تهديدات محدّدة	analysis of the probability and impact of identified threats
تقييم تهديد	threat assessment
منتج استخباراتيّ قائم على تحليل تهديد	intelligence product based on a threat analysis
نغمة	tone
وجهة نظر إيجابيّة أو سلبيّة تضعها وسائل إعلام أو كيان آخر عن قصّة ما	positive or negative slant the media or other entity puts on a story

اتِّجاه	trend
اتِّجاه عامَ لسير الأحداث	general direction in which events are moving
عدم اليقين	uncertainty
شكوك متأصّلة في بيئة ذات معرفة محدودةً أو ناقصة	doubts inherent in an environment of limited or imperfect knowledge
تحليل الضّعف	vulnerability analysis
عمليّة تحليل نشاط أو تنظيم من وجهة نظر عدوّ لتحديد نقاط الضّعف الخاصّة بها	process of analyzing an activity or organization from the perspective of an adversary to identify its own vulnerabilities

3. HUMAN INTELLIGENCE (HUMINT)

إمكانيّة الوصول	access
حدود وصول المصدر إلى معلومات مطلوبة	degree to which a source has access to desired information
عميل الوصول (إلى هدف محتمل بهدف تجنيده أو تقييم وضعه)	access agent
فرد تسمح له علاقاته بالوصول إلى هدف	individual whose relationships allow him/her to access a target
أتباع	adherents
أفراد يتعاونون مع أو يسعون إلى تنفيذ أعمال عنف نيابة عن منظّمة إرهابيّة	individuals who collaborate with or seek to carry out acts of violence on behalf of a terrorist organization

عميل	agent
شخص مجنّد لجمع معلومات لصالح وكالة؛ يشير مصطلح «عميل» بشكل عامّ إلى مصدر غير تابع للوكالة؛ ومع ذلك، تستخدم بعض الدّوائر مصطلح «عميل» للإشارة إلى موظّفين تابعين للوكالة أيضاً	person recruited to collect information for an agency; generally, "agent" refers to a source who is not an employee of the agency; however, some services also use the term "agent" to refer to employees of the agency
تقييم عميل	agent assessment
تقرير حول أداء عميل	report about an agent's performance
تطوير عميل	agent development
تطوير علاقة مع شخص لديه إمكانيّة الوصول إلى معلومات مطلوبة بقصد تجنيده كعميل	developing a relationship with a person with access to desired information with the intent of recruiting him/her as an agent
عميل في الدّاخل	agent in place
فرد يعمل داخل مؤسّسة استخبار اتيّة بتوجيه من جهة معادية	individual working within an intelligence organization under the direction of a hostile service

شبكة العميل	agent net
مجموعة من العملاء منظّمة حول عميل رئيسيّ بوجه عامّ	group of agents generally organized around a principal agent
عميل ذو تأثير	agent of influence
عميل موجَّه لاستخدام منصبه للتَّأثير على الرَّأي العامّ أو السِّياسات	agent directed to use his/her position to influence public opinion or policies
عميل محرّض	agent provocateur
عميل هدفه التَّودَد إلى مجموعة وتحريض تلك المجموعة على أفعال ستؤدّي إلى عواقب سلبيّة على المجموعة	agent whose goal is to ingratiate himself with a group and incite that group to actions that will result in negative consequences for the group
إنهاء (خدمة) العميل	agent termination
إنهاء العلاقة الوظيفيّة مع عميل	ending the employment relationship with an agent
اسم مستعار	alias
هويّة مزيّفة	fake identity

تحقّق من صحّة مصدر موجّه	asset validation
عمليّة تُستخدَم لتحديد درجة أمانة المصدر الموجَّه والثّقة به والفائدة منه ودرجة خضوعه لسيطرة ضابط الحالة	process to determine the degree to which an asset is authentic, reliable, useful and under the case officer's control
لجوء	asylum
حماية مقدَّمة لمواطن أجنبيّ يواجه اضطهاداً في بلده	protection offered to a foreign national who faces persecution in his/her home country
أجواء	atmospherics
معلومات عن جوّ أو مزاج مجموعة من النّاس	information about the atmosphere or mood of a people group
سند	backstop
ترتيبات معيّنة بغرض إثبات قصّة غطاء	arrangements made to substantiate a cover story
قائمة سوداء	black list
قائمة الأفراد الّذين يُعتبَر إلقاء القبض عليهم أولويّة	list of individuals whose capture is a priority

ابتزاز	blackmail
استخدام معلومات سلبيّة عن فرد لإجباره على العمل نيابة عن جهاز استخبارات معادٍ	using derogatory information about an individual to coerce him/her to act on behalf of an adversarial intelligence service
استخبارات السّيرة الذّاتيّة	biographical intelligence
استخبارات حول أشخاص أجانب ذوي أهمّيّة	intelligence about foreign persons of interest
تأثير متعلّق بسيرة ذاتيّة	biographic leverage
شكل من أشكال الابتزاز الّذي تُستخدَم فيه معلومات عن فرد كقوّة ضغط لإجباره أن يفعل شيئاً معيّناً	a form of blackmail in which information about an individual is used as leverage to coerce him/her to do something
قياسات حيويّة	biometrics
كشف صفات جسديّة فريدة من نوعها لتحديد هويّة فرد	detection of unique physical traits to identify an individual
استخبارات قائمة على قياسات حيويّة	biometrics-enabled intelligence (BEI)
استخبارات مستمدّة من تواقيع حيويّة	intelligence derived from biometric signatures

قائمة مراقبة مزوّدة بقياسات حيويّة	Biometrics-Enabled Watch List (BEWL)
قائمة بأفراد ذوي اهتمام محدّدين بصورة حيويّة يجب اتّخاذ إجراءات محدّدة عند مواجهتهم	list of biometrically identified individuals of interest with pre-scribed actions to be taken if encountered
حسن النّيّة	bona fides
تحديد أنّ هويّة فرد صحيحة كما يدّعيها	determination that an individual is who he or she claims to be
مواجهة وجيزة	brief encounter
اتّصال قصير بين الضّابط المسؤول عن القضيّة والعميل	brief contact between a case officer and agent
التقاء عرضيّ	bump
مواجهة مفتعلة مع فرد لتبدو كأنّها عشوائيّة	encounter with an indi-vidual contrived to appear random
ضابط القضيّة	case officer
محترف استخباراتيّ مسؤول عن التّعامل مع القضايا والمصادر الموجّهة	intelligence profes-sional responsible for handling cases and assets

طعام الدّجاج   chicken feed

معلومات غير هامّة مقدّمة لعدوّ من أجل كسب ثقة هذا العدوّ بالعميل المزدوج الّذي يقدّم المعلومات (*أنظر مادّة التّغذية*)   inconsequential information provided to an adversary in order to gain the adversary's trust in the double agent delivering the information (*see also* feed material)

معتقلون مدنيّون   civilian internees

مدنيّون محتجزون في وقت الحرب   civilians detained in war time

اسم رمزيّ   code name

اسم مستعار مستخدم لإخفاء هويّة ناشط   alias used to conceal an operative's identity

رمية باردة   cold pitch

اقتراب من هدف للتّوظيف دون اتّصال مسبق أو تطوير   approaching a target for recruitment without prior contact or development

مصدر سرّيّ   confidential source

مصدر يوفّر معلومات مع التّوقّع بأنّ المعلومات و/أو العلاقة ستبقى سرّيّة   source who provides information with the expectation that the information and/or relationship will be kept confidential

عميل الإرباك	confusion agent
عميل موجّه لإرباك استخبارات عدوّ	agent dispatched to confuse an adversary's intelligence service
عميل متعاقد	contract agent
عميل موظّف لمرّة أو عدّة مرّات لمشاريع محدّدة	agent hired once or multiple times for specific projects
تحكّم	control
قدرة ضابط قضيّة على السّيطرة على عميل	case officer's ability to control an agent
عميل خاضع للسّيطرة	controlled agent
عميل تحت سيطرة جهاز استخبارات	agent under the control of an intelligence service
مصدر خاضع للسّيطرة	controlled source
مصدر تحت سيطرة جهاز استخباراتيّ	source under the control of an intelligence service
مراسل متعاون	cooperative contact
مصدر موجّه يؤدّي بعض الأنشطة لجهاز استخبارات إلّا أنّه لا يرغب في الخضوع لسيطرة ذلك الجهاز	asset who performs some activities for an intelligence service but is unwilling to be controlled by that service

معتقل متعاون	cooperative detainee
معتقل له سجلّ من الإجابات الصّادقة على الأسئلة	detainee with a record of truthfully answering questions
ساعٍ	courier
شخص يحمل معلومات من نقطة إلى أخرى	person who carries information from one point to another
غطاء	cover
وظيفة مستخدمة لإخفاء أنشطة استخبارات شخص ما	position used to conceal a person's intelligence activities
غطاء الفعل	cover for action
سبب منطقيّ لممارسة نشاط معيّن	logical reason for doing a particular activity
غطاء الحالة	cover for status
سبب منطقيّ للتّواجد في مكان معيّن	logical reason for being in a particular place
اسم غطاء	cover name
اسم مستخدم لإخفاء الهويّة الحقيقيّة لفرد أو لأيّ كيان آخر	name used to conceal the true identity of an individual or other entity

منظّمة غطاء	cover organization
منظّمة وهميّة وُضعت لتوفير غطاء لعميل أو ناشط	fake organization crafted to provide cover for an agent or operative
توقّف غطائيّ (تمويهيّ)	cover stop
وقفة للتّظاهر بأنّ هدف الرّحلة بريء	stop made to make the purpose of a trip appear innocent
قصّة غطاء	cover story
قصّة خلفيّة لإثبات غطاء فرد	background story to substantiate an individual's cover
أوراق اعتماد	credentials
وثائق تحدّد صاحبها ممثّلاً عن وكالة حكوميّة	documents identifying the holder as a representative of a government agency
زراعة	cultivation
إقامة علاقة مع مصدر محتمل للمعلومات	establishing a relationship with a potential source of information
مقابلة في الحجز	custodial interview
مقابلة معتقل أو سجين	interview of a detainee or prisoner

cut out   انقطاع

intermediary used to prevent direct contact between certain individuals   وسيط مستخدم لمنع الاتّصال المباشر بين أفراد معيّنين

dancer   راقص

detainee who goes through cycles of resistance and cooperation with his/her interrogators   معتقل أحياناً يقاوم وأحياناً يتعاون مع من يستجوبه

danger signals   إشارات خطر

signal between individuals to indicate danger from or exposure to an adversary   إشارة بين أفراد للإشارة إلى خطرٍ من عدوَ أو انكشافَ لعدوَ

debrief   استجواب

to question an individual about a recent operation or experience   استجواب فرد عن عمليّة أخيرة أو تجربة أخيرة

معلن declared

فرد معترف رسمياً بانتمائه إلى individual whose affilia-
وكالة استخبارات لدى tion with an intelli-
حكومة البلد الّذي يعمل فيه gence agency is for-
mally acknowledged
to the government of
the country in which
he/she is operating

غطاء عميق deep cover

غطاء مصمّم لتحمّل تمحيص cover designed to with-
دقيق stand intense scrutiny

ارتداد defection

تحويل الولاء من دولة لأخرى shifting loyalty from
one country to an-
other

منشقّ defector

فرد يتخلّى عن الولاء لبلده individual who aban-
dons loyalty to
his/her country

حرفيّة المنطقة المرفوضة denied area tradecraft

منهجيّة التّعامل مع عملاء في methodology for han-
بيئات معادية dling agents in hostile
environments

تطوير develop

أنظر تطوير عميل *see* agent development

معلومات انتقاصيّة	derogatory information
معلومات تقوّض مصداقيّة أو ولاء فرد ما	information that undermines an individual's credibility or loyalty
حرفان متتاليان	digraph
حروف رمزيّة مستخدمة للإشارة إلى دولة العمل الخاصّة بعميل	code letters used to indicate an agent's country of operation
غطاء دبلوماسيّ	diplomatic cover
لقب دبلوماسيّ يُعطى لضابط استخبارات سرّيّ كغطاء	diplomatic title given to a clandestine intelligence officer as cover
حصانة دبلوماسيّة	diplomatic immunity
حصانة الضّبّاط الدّبلوماسيّين من الملاحقة القضائيّة في دول مستقبِلة	immunity of diplomatic officers from prosecution in receiving states
وصول مباشر	direct access
حصول على المعلومات مباشرةً	firsthand access to information
شخص ساخط	disaffected person
فرد يُبعَد عن أو يفتقر إلى الولاء لبلده	individual who is alienated from or lacking loyalty to his/her country

إغفال	discards
عملاء أو ضبّاط تفضحهم الوكالة الخاصّة بهم عمداً لصرف انتباه الخصم عن هدف ذي قيمة أعلى	agents or officers deliberately compromised by their agency to distract an adversary's attention from a higher value target
تخلّص	disposal
قطع العلاقات مع عميل	cutting ties with an agent
ملفّ	dossier
ملفّ معلومات عن فرد	file of information about an individual
مواطن مزدوج	dual citizen
فرد يُعتبَر مواطناً لبلدين أو أكثر	individual who is a citizen of two or more countries
معلومات الاستنتاج	educing information (EI)
المناهج المختلفة لانتزاع معلومات من مصادر بشريّة	the various approaches to elicit information from human sources

elicitation استنباط

acquiring information from an individual in a manner that does not reveal the interviewer's intent

حصول على معلومات من فرد بطريقة لا تكشف عن نيّة الشّخص الّذي يجري المقابلة

émigré مهاجر

individual who lawfully leaves his country to resettle in another country

فرد يترك بلده على نحو قانونيّ لإعادة توطينه في بلد آخر

established source مصدر مؤسَّس

source who has previously provided information and is believed to be reliable

مصدر قدّم معلومات سابقاً ويُعتقَد أنّه ذو موثوقيّة

exchange commodity سلعة التّبادل

something other than money with which an agent is paid

شيء آخر غير المال يُدفع للعميل

fabricator ملفق

individual or group who fabricates or inflates information

فرد أو مجموعة تلفق أو تضخّم معلومات

تجنيد العلم المزيف	false-flag recruitment
تجنيد فرد يعتقد أنّه يعمل لبلد ما ولكنّه في الواقع يعمل لحساب بلد مختلف	recruiting an individual who believes he or she is working for one country but is in fact working for a different country
مادّة التّغذية	feed material
معلومات غير هامّة مقدّمة لعدوّ من أجل كسب ثقة الخصم بالعميل المزدوج الّذي يقدّم المعلومات (أنظر طعام الدّجاج)	inconsequential information provided to an adversary in order to gain the adversary's trust in the double agent delivering the information (see also chicken feed)
كاتب عامود خامس	fifth columnist
فرد يعمل لتقويض بلده أو مجموعته ولديه تعاطف سرّيَ مع عدوَ	individual who acts to undermine his/her country or group out of secret sympathy with an enemy
عائم	floater
فرد يؤدّي خدمات عرضيّة لجهاز استخباراتيّ وأحياناً دون قصد	individual who performs occasional services for an intelligence service, sometimes unwittingly

foreign contact	اتّصال خارجيّ
contact with a foreign national	اتّصال بمواطن أجنبيّ
foreign intelligence entity (FIE)	كيان استخبارات خارجيّة
foreign individual or group or organization known or suspected to conduct intelligence operations against a specific state	فرد أو جماعة أو منظّمة أجنبيّة معروفة أو مشكوكة بإجراء عمليّات استخباراتيّة ضدّ دولة معيّنة
front	جبهة
ostensibly legitimate organization established to provide cover for agents or officers	منظّمة شرعيّة ظاهريّاً أنشئت لتوفير غطاء لعملاء أو ضبّاط
front organization	منظّمة أماميّة
ostensibly legitimate organization established to provide cover for agents or officers	منظّمة شرعيّة ظاهريّاً أنشئت لتوفير غطاء لعملاء أو ضبّاط
ghosts	أشباح
detainees whose existence is denied	معتقلون غير معترف بوجودهم

قائمة رماديّة   grey list

قائمة أفراد لديهم إمكانيّة الوصول إلى معلومات لكنّ دوافعهم السّياسيّة غير معروفة   list of individuals with access to information, but whose political motivations are unknown

مقايضة   greymail

تهديدات بالكشف عن معلومات حسّاسة أو مصنّفة لإرغام حكومة على إسقاط تهم قانونيّة ضدّ فرد   threats to reveal sensitive or classified information to coerce a government to drop legal charges against an individual

الرّجل الرّماديّ   the grey man

جاسوس ذو مظهر عادٍ لا يجذب الانتباه   a spy with a nondescript appearance which does not attract attention

مسيّس   handler

ضابط مسؤول عن أنشطة مصدر موجّه أو مصدر   officer responsible for the activities of an asset or source

فخّ العسل   honey trap

عمليّة استخدام الجنس للإيقاع بهدف   operation using sex to entrap a target

مجال بشريّ	human domain
كافّة جوانب محيط مجموعة ما المؤثّرة على السّلوك البشريّ	all aspects of a group's environment that impact human behavior
استخبارات بشريّة	human intelligence (HUMINT)
استخبارات مجمَّعة من مصادر بشريّة	intelligence collected from human sources
مصدر بشريّ	human source
فرد يقدّم معلومات	individual who provides information
جامع الاستخبارات البشريّة	HUMINT collector
فرد يجمع معلومات من مصادر بشريّة	individual who collects information from human sources
مصدر الاستخبارات البشريّة	HUMINT source
فرد يقدّم المعلومات	individual who provides information
استهداف الاستخبارات البشريّة	HUMINT targeting
تحديد وتطوير مصادر الاستخبارات البشريّة	identifying and developing HUMINT sources

غير قانونيّ	illegal
ضابط سرّيّ يعمل بصورة غير قانونيّة في بلد أجنبيّ	clandestine officer operating illegally within a foreign country
اتّصالات غير شخصيّة	impersonal communication
تواصل دون احتكاك جسديّ	communication with no physical contact
وصول غير مباشر	indirect access
حصول على معلومات بطريقة غير مباشرة	secondhand access to information
ارتداد محفّز	induced defection
إقناع مسؤول بالانشقاق	persuading an official to defect
تسلّل	infiltration
وضع عميل أو ضابط ضمن منطقة مستهدفة	positioning an agent or officer within a target area
مخبر	informant
فرد يقدّم معلومات لجهاز استخباراتيّ	individual who provides information to an intelligence service

inside man رجل في الدّاخل

intelligence officer working in a foreign country under the cover of his foreign ministry ضابط استخباراتيّ يعمل في بلد أجنبيّ تحت غطاء وزارة خارجيّة بلده

insider شخص داخليّ

individual with authorized access to a service فرد يمتلك تصريحاً بالوصول إلى جهاز

insider threat تهديد من الدّاخل

individual who uses or attempts to use insider access to harm a service فرد يستخدم أو يحاول استخدام شخص مطّلع على الأسرار الدّاخليّة لجهاز ليضرّ به

interrogation استجواب

questioning a detainee to obtain information استجواب معتقل للحصول على معلومات

lead تمهيد

potential source of information مصدر محتمل للمعلومات

قانونيّ legal

ضابط استخباراتيّ يعمل علناً لحكومته في بلد أجنبيّ إلّا أنّ نشاطاته الاستخباراتيّة سرّيّة — intelligence officer who works openly for his/ her government in a foreign country but whose intelligence activities are covert

ملحق قانونيّ legal attaché (legat)

عملاء مكتب التّحقيقات الفيدراليّة المعيّنون في السّفارات الأميركيّة في الخارج — FBI agents assigned to overseas US embassies

إقامة قانونيّة legal residency

ضابط استخبارات في بلد أجنبيّ معروف بأنّه ممثّل الحكومة إلّا أنّ انتماءه لجهاز استخبارات ليس معروفاً بالضّرورة — intelligence officer in a foreign country who is identified as a government representative but whose affiliation with an intelligence service is not necessarily identified

مسافر قانونيّ legal traveler

فرد يحمل وثائق سفر شرعيّة — individual with legitimate travel documentation

أسطورة	legend
قصّة غطاء لناشط	an operative's cover story
شرعيّ	legitimate
وصف يُستخدَم لفرد يدّعي هويّته الصّحيحة	description used for an individual who is what he or she claims to be
مصنوع	made
مصطلح يُستخدم لوصف مراقب تمّ تحديده من قبل الفرد المتابع له	term used to describe a surveillant who has been identified by the individual he or she is following
دوافع الانشقاق المشتركة	MICE
اختصار لأربعة دوافع مشتركة للانشقاق: المال والإيديولوجية والإكراه والغرور	acronym for four common motivations for defection: money, ideology, coercion, ego
حافز	motivation
عوامل تحفّز فرداً على الانشقاق	factors that incentivize an individual to defect

تحليل الحركات	movements analysis
مراقبة مسؤولين للتَمييز بين دبلوماسيّين شرعيّين وجواسيس	surveillance of officials to distinguish legiti-mate diplomats from spies
تعقَّب اسم	name trace
بحث عن معلومات حول فرد	search for information about an individual
غطاء غير رسميّ	non-official cover (NOC)
ضابط يعمل في بلد أجنبيّ دون غطاء حكوميّ أو دبلوماسيّ	officer operating in a foreign country with-out government or diplomatic cover
شذرة	nugget
مصطلح بريطانيّ يعبّر عن شيء مقدَّم لفرد لإقناعه بالانشقاق	British term for some-thing offered to an individual to persuade him/her to defect
غطاء تنظيميّ	organizational cover
حصول على وظيفة لدى عمل شرعيّ كغطاء لأنشطة سرّية	obtaining employment with a legitimate business as cover for covert activities

رجل في الخارج   outside man

ضابط استخباراتيّ يعمل في بلد
أجنبيّ دون غطاء من
حكومته
   intelligence officer
working in a foreign
country without cover
from his government

تجنيد ورقيّ   paper recruitment

تجنيد عملاء عديمي الفائدة أو
وهميّين
   recruitment of useless
or imaginary agents

اختراق   penetration

حصول بشكل سرّيّ على
إمكانيّة الوصول إلى جهاز
استخباراتيّ أجنبيّ
   clandestinely obtaining
access to a foreign
intelligence service

اجتماع شخصيّ   personal meeting

لقاء شخصيّ بين مسيّس
ومصدر موجّه
   in-person meeting
between a handler
and asset

شخصيّة غير مرغوب بها   persona non grata (PNG)

شخص طُرد و/أو محظور من
دخول بلد نتيجة الانخراط
في أنشطة تتعارض مع
الوضع الدّبلوماسيّ وغالباً
ما تنطوي على التّجسّس
   a person evicted from
and/or prohibited
from entering a coun-
try as a result of
engaging in activities
inconsistent with dip-
lomatic status, often
involving espionage

رمية	pitch
محاولة لتوظيف مصدر موجّه	attempt to recruit an asset
تنسيب	placement
قرب من معلومات مطلوبة	proximity to desired information
سباكة	plumbing
دعم تشغيليّ لتمكين عميل أو ضابط من العمل في بلد أجنبيّ	operational support enabling an agent or officer to operate in a foreign country
قمامة الجيب	pocket litter
موادّ موجودة في جيب عميل أو ضابط يمكن استغلالها للحصول على معلومات أو موادّ موضوعة في جيب عميل أو ضابط لتعزيز قصّة غطاء	items in an agent's or officer's pocket that can be exploited to obtain information, or items placed in an agent's or officer's pocket to reinforce a cover story
جهاز كشف الكذب	polygraph
اختبار كشف الكذب	lie-detector test

فحص إيجابيّ	positive vetting
مصطلح بريطانيّ لفحص أفراد لديهم إمكانيّة الوصول إلى معلومات مصنّفة	British term for screening individuals with access to classified information
تحقيق أوّليّ	preliminary investigation
تحقيق أوّليّ لبيان حقيقة شخص لم يتمّ التّأكد من تورّطه في أنشطة إجراميّة	initial investigation of a target whose involvement in criminal activities is uncertain
إجراء مقابلة كعذر	pretext interview
محادثة تكون ظاهريّاً حول موضوع ما لإخفاء الغرض الحقيقيّ من المقابلة	conversation which is ostensibly about one topic to disguise the true purpose of the interview
عميل رئيسيّ	principal agent (PA)
عميل يتلقّى التّدريب المعمّق ومهمّته تجنيد عملاء إضافيّين وتدريبهم	agent who receives in-depth training whose job it is to recruit and train additional agents
تـهيئة السّباكة	putting in the plumbing
وضع الدّعم التّشغيليّ موضع التّنفيذ لتمكين عمليّة في الخارج	putting operational support in place to enable an overseas operation

تجنيد	recruitment
جهود لفرض السّيطرة على مواطن أجنبيّ كمصدر للاستخبارات	efforts to establish control over a foreign national as a source of intelligence
دورة التّجنيد	recruitment cycle
عمليّة تجنيد المصدر الموجّه	process for recruiting assets
برنامج إعادة التّوطين	resettlement program
برنامج لإعادة توطين منشقّين وأسرهم لحمايتهم	program to resettle defectors and their families for their protection
عائد	returnee
فرد يعود بملء إرادته إلى موطنه السّابق	individual who willingly returns to his/her former homeland
فحص	screening
تقييم فرد لتحديد قيمته المحتملة	evaluating an individual to determine his/her potential value
تجسس باستخدام الجنس	sexpionage
استخدام الجنس والشّهوة لجمع معلومات استخباراتيّة	the use of sex and lust to collect intelligence information

مفرد	singleton
عميل يعمل بمفرده	agent who operates alone
عميل نائم	sleeper
عميل غير نشط موضوع في موقع الهدف من أجل نشاط مستقبليّ	non-active agent placed in a target location for future activation
سترة الواشي	snitch jacket
اتّهام هدف بأنّه مخبر من أجل تدمير مصداقيّته	accusing a target of being an informant in order to destroy his/her credibility
ملفّات ناعمة	soft files
ملفّات غير رسميّة تحتوي على معلومات عن عادات الموظّفين الشّخصيّة وارتباطاتهم	unofficial files containing information about employees' personal habits and associations
مباع	sold
مصطلح مستخدم لوصف عميل خانه جهازه الاستخباراتيّ عمداً	term used to describe an agent whose service has intentionally betrayed him/her

مصدر source

فرد يقدّم معلومات لجهاز
استخباراتيّ

individual who provides
information to an
intelligence service

إدارة مصدر source management

مراقبة استخدام المصادر
لضمان أمن عمليّة معيّنة

monitoring the use of
sources to ensure the
security of an opera-
tion

تسجيل مصدر source registry

فهرس المصادر المستخدمة
لإدارة المصادر وتجنّب
الازدواجيّة في النّهج

catalog of sources used
to manage sources
and avoid duplication
of approaches

تحقّق من صحّة المصدر source validation

عمليّة فحص مصدر

process of vetting a
source

شبح spook

جاسوس spy

تحديد spot

تحديد مرشّحين محتملين
لتجنّدهم خدمة معيّنة

to identify potential
candidates for recruit-
ment by a service

راصد   spotter

فرد معيّن لتحديد المرشّحين   individual assigned to
المحتمل تجنيدهم   identify potential
candidates for
recruitment

جاسوس   spy

ضابط أو مصدر موجّه أو   intelligence officer, as-
عميل أو مصدر استخباراتيَ   set, agent, or source

مراسل استخباراتيَ   stringer

عميل مستقلّ يمرّر معلومات   freelance agent who
يحصل عليها إلى جهاز   passes on information
استخباراتيَ   he or she obtains to
an intelligence ser-
vice

عميل دعم   support agent

عميل يقدّم دعماً لوجستيّاً   agent who provides
لعمليّة   logistical support for
an operation

راصد مواهب   talent spotter

عميل مكلّف بتحديد مجنّدين   agent tasked with iden-
محتملين   tifying potential
recruits

دراسة هدف	target study
تجميع كلّ المعلومات المتاحة لجهاز الاستخبارات عن تجنيد محتمل	collection of all information available to the intelligence service about a potential recruit
خيانة	treason
خيانة شخص لبلده	betraying one's country
خائن	traitor
فرد يخون بلده	individual who betrays his/her country
حوّل	turn
إجبار عميل خصم أو إقناعه بأن ينشقّ أو يصبح عميلاً مزدوجاً	coerce or persuade an adversarial agent to defect or become a double agent
غير معلن	undeclared
فرد ذو انتماء غير معلن إلى وكالة استخباراتيّة	individual whose intelligence agency affiliation is not declared

unilateral	أحاديّ الجانب
agent who works under the control of an agency but has no visible connection to the agency or to his/her government	عميل يعمل تحت سيطرة وكالة ولكن ليس لديه اتّصال ظاهر مع الوكالة أو حكومته
unwitting	جاهل
unaware that a cover story disguises an underlying intelligence connection or activity	جاهل بأنَ قصّة غطاء تخفي حقيقة اتّصالات أو أنشطة استخباراتيّة كامنة
vacuum cleaner	مكنسة كهربائيّة
term used to describe a source who passes along every piece of information he or she learns regardless of its relevance	مصطلح مستخدم لوصف مصدر يمرّر كلّ معلومة يحصل عليها بغضّ النّظر عن صلتها
vetting	تدقيق
evaluating an asset to determine veracity, reliability and control	تقييم مصدر موجّه لتحديد المصداقيّة والموثوقيّة والسّيطرة
volunteer	متطوّع
individual who initiates contact with an agency to volunteer information	فرد يبادر بالاتّصال بوكالة لتقديم معلومات

walk-in قادم / مباشر

individual who initiates contact with an agency to volunteer information

فرد يبادر بالاتّصال بوكالة لتقديم معلومات

white list قائمة بيضاء

list of individuals who are expected to have access to desired information

قائمة الأفراد المتوقّع إمكانيّة وصولهم إلى معلومات مطلوبة

witting بارع

aware that a cover story disguises an underlying intelligence connection or activity

على علم بأنّ قصّة غطاء تخفي حقيقة اتّصالات أو أنشطة استخباراتيّة مستترة

4. OPERATIONS

إحباط	abort
إنهاء عمليّة	to terminate an operation
تدابير نشطة	active measures
عمل سرّيّ	covert action
التّحريض والدّعاية	agit-prop
دعاية باستخدام الفنّ أو الصّور المثيرة لجذب انتباه وسائل الإعلام	propaganda using art or dramatic images to attract media attention [derived from "agitation" and "propaganda"]
لقاء بديل	alternate meet
لقاء تمّ سلفاً التّرتيب لعقده في وقت ومكان محدّدين إذا فُوّت اللّقاء المجدول بانتظام	a meeting pre-arranged to take place at a set time and place if a regularly scheduled meeting is missed
اعتقال	apprehension
حجز فرد	taking an individual into custody

تقييم منطقة	area assessment
معلومات تمّ جمعها عن منطقة بعد التسلّل	information collected about an area after infiltration
دراسة منطقة	area study
معلومات تمّ جمعها عن منطقة قبل دخول المنطقة	information collected about an area before entering the area
اغتيال	assassination
جريمة قتل شخص بارز بدافع سياسيّ	politically motivated murder of a prominent person
التقاط مساعد بواسطة سيّارة	assisted car pick-up
التقاط حيث يقوم ضابط بالقيادة، بينما ضابط ثانٍ يستجوب مصدراً	pick-up in which one officer drives while another debriefs a source
قاعدة	base
موقع أصغر من محطّة استخباراتيّة	a post smaller than a station
منارة	beacon
جهاز موصول بجسم لتتبّع موقعه	device attached to an object to track its location

عمليّة ثنائيّة	bilateral operation
عمليّة منفّذة بالتّنسيق مع جهاز استخباراتيّ أجنبيّ أو جهاز استخباراتيّ آخر من نفس البلد	operation carried out in coordination with a foreign intelligence service or with another intelligence service of the same country
أسود	black
مبهم؛ لا تستهدفه مراقبة معادية	inconspicuous; not under hostile surveillance
عمليّات الحقيبة السّوداء	black bag operations
عمليّات سرّيّة تنطوي على الكسر والدّخول	clandestine operations involving breaking and entering
صندوق أسود	black box
جهاز تسجيل يُستخدَم للتّجسّس	recording device used for espionage
تزوير أسود	black forgery
مادّة أُنشئت لتبدو وكـأنّها قد صدرت عن عدوّ	material created to appear to have originated from an enemy

عمليّات سوداء	black operations
عمليّات حسّاسة للغاية	very sensitive operations
دعاية سوداء	black propaganda
دعاية نشرها طرف معيّن إلّا أنّها صُنِعت لتظهر كما لو أنّها صدرت عن عدوّ	propaganda disseminated by one party but made to appear as though it originated from an adversary
متدرّبون سود	black trainees
رعايا أجانب أُحضِروا إلى الولايات المتّحدة للتّدرّب دون أن يعرفوا في أيّ بلد يتواجدون	foreign nationals brought to the US for training without knowing in what country they are located
مكشوف	blown
فضح؛ كشف هويّة فرد معيّن (أنظر محروق)	exposure, having one's identity revealed (*see also* burnt)
وثائق ملزمة	bound documents
كتب مجلّدة بطريقة معيّنة لضمان أنّ إزالة صفحات منه ستؤدّي إلى ضرر ظاهر للكتاب	books bound in such a way to ensure that removing pages will result in visible damage to the book

غسل الدَماغ	brainwashing
إقناع فرد بتبنّي مجموعة مختلفة من المعتقدات قسراً	coercively persuading an individual to adopt a different set of beliefs
تمرير فُرشاة	brush pass
لقاء وجيز حيث يتمّ تمرير شيء من شخص إلى آخر	a brief encounter in which an item is passed from one person to the other
جهاز تنصّت	bug
جهاز تنصّت مخبّأ	concealed listening device
تحت التّنصّت	bugged
وصف مكان أو شيء يحتوي على جهاز تنصّت مخبّأ	description of an area or object containing a concealed listening device
حقيبة حرق	burn bag
حاوية تحمل وثائق حسّاسة لتدمَّر	container which holds sensitive documents to be destroyed

إشعار الإحراق	burn notice
بيان من قبل وكالة استخباراتيّة لأخرى أنّه لا يمكن الاعتماد على فرد أو مجموعة معيّنة	statement from one agency to another that a person or group is unreliable
محروق	burnt
فضـح؛ كشف هويّة فرد معيّن (أنظر مكشوف)	exposure, having one's identity revealed (*see also* blown)
دفن	bury
إخفاء معلومات سرّيّة في نصّ رسالة	to hide secret information within the text of a communication
كابلات	cables
رسائل بين مكاتب ميدانيّة وقيادة عامّة	messages between field offices and headquarters
حملة	campaign
سلسلة من العمليّات لتحقيق هدف	series of operations to accomplish an objective
كربون	carbons
ورقة معالجة كيميائيّاً تحتوي على كتابة غير مرئيّة	chemically treated paper containing invisible writing

التقاط بواسطة سيّارة   car pick-up

التقاط حيث يقوم ضابط بتحميل مصدر ويجري معه اجتماعاً في سيّارة   pick-up in which an officer picks up a source and interviews him/her in a vehicle

رمي من سيّارة   car toss

رمي سرّيّ لشيء من سيّارة متحرّكة على مكان معيّن   clandestinely tossing an item from a moving car at a designated location

قضيّة   case

عمليّة استخباراتيّة   intelligence operation

موت قضيّة   case death

عمليّة تفشل دون سبب محدّد   operation which fails for no identified reason

غلاف   casing

مراقبة سرّيّة لمنطقة   clandestine surveillance of an area

نقطة الاختناق / عقدة حرجة   choke point/critical node

النّقطة الّتي تحتاج لأقلّ جهد لتقدّم أكبر قدر من التّأثير   point where minimum effort delivers maximum impact

سرّيّة	clandestine
منجز بسرّيّة	done in secrecy
تجميع سرّيّ	clandestine collection
حصول على معلومات بقصد إخفاء وجود عمليّة	acquisition of information with the intent to conceal the existence of the operation
عمليّة سرّيّة مقارنة بعمليّة مغطّاة	clandestine vs. covert operation
عمليّات مغطّاة تخفي الكفيل أو النّيّة	covert operations conceal the sponsor or intent
عمليّات سرّيّة تخفي العمليّة نفسها	clandestine operations conceal the operation itself
نظيف	clean
لا رقابة عليه	free from surveillance
تجميع	collection
جمع معلومات استخباراتيّة	gathering intelligence
جامع	collector
شخص يجمع معلومات استخباراتيّة	person who gathers intelligence

معلومات استخباراتيّة قتاليّة	combat intelligence
معلومات مطلوبة عن عدوّ لدعم عمليّات عسكريّة	information about an enemy required to support military operations
إسقاط تجاريّ	commercial drop
مكان عمل تجاريّ حيث يمكن للعملاء والضّبّاط تسليم أو التقاط رسائل	a business at which agents and officers can drop off or pick up messages
متابعة مخفيّة	concealed monitoring
استخدام التّكنولوجيا لمراقبة هدف خلسةً	the use of technology to surreptitiously monitor a target
جهاز إخفاء	concealment device
جهاز مصمّم لإخفاء و/أو نقل موادّ سرّاً	device designed to hide and/or secretly transfer materials
قنوات	conduits
نقاط الدّخول إلى هدف محدّد	entry points to an identified target

طيران محيطيّ	contour flying
طائرة تحلّق على مقربة من سطح الأرض (في كثير من الأحيان للاستطلاع أو لتجنّب الكشف)	aircraft flying close to the surface of the earth (often for reconnaissance or to avoid detection)
تطويق وبحث	cordon and search
تقنيّة مكافحة التّمرّد عن طريق عزل مجموعة أو منطقة للبحث عن موادّ مستهدفة أو أشخاص مستهدفين	counterinsurgency technique of isolating a group or area for the purposes of searching for targeted material or people
مكافحة استطلاع العدوّ	counterreconnaissance
تدابير لمنع مراقبة منطقة من قبل عدوّ	measures to prevent observation of an area by an adversary
تغطية	coverage
تواجد وكالة في منطقة معيّنة	an agency's presence in a given area
مخفيّ	covert
مصمّمة لإخفاء كفيل أو نيّة عمليّة	designed to conceal the sponsor or intent of an operation

عمل مخفيّ covert action

أنشطة سرّيَة للتَأثير على الوضع السّياسيّ في بلد أجنبيّ covert activities to influence the political situation in a foreign country

قناة سرّيّة covert channel

قناة اتّصال سرّيّة secret communication channel

تقديم تقرير موجز لتقييم الضّرر damage assessment debriefing

تقديم تقرير موجز يلي فضح عمليّة debriefing following a compromised operation

سيطرة على الضّرر damage control

تدابير للحدّ من الضّرر النّاجم عن عمليّة فاشلة measures to minimize the damage caused by an aborted operation

إسقاط ميّت dead drop

مكان سرّيّ حيث يمكن لعميل أن يترك شيئاً ليلتقطه المسيّس في وقت لاحق (أنظر إسقاط رسالة) secret unattended location where an agent can leave something for pickup by his/her handler at a later time (see also letter drop)

خداع	decoy
شيء مزيّف يشبه شيئاً حقيقيّاً	fake object resembling a real object
منطقة مرفوضة	denied area
منطقة واقعة تحت سيطرة عدوَ	area under enemy control
زعزعة الاستقرار	destabilization
عمل سرّيّ يهدف إلى تقويض حكومة وزعزعة استقرار بلد	covert action aimed at undermining a government and destabilizing a country
دليل مباشر	direct evidence
معلومات تثبت أو تدحض شيئاً ما	information that verifies or disproves something
قذر	dirty
يصف عمليّة أو فرداً قد انكشف	describes an operation or individual who has been exposed
تنظيف جافّ	dry cleaning
تدابير للتفادي من أو كشف مراقبة	measures to avoid or detect surveillance

تنصَّت	eavesdropping
الاستماع سرّاً إلى محادثة	secretly listening to a conversation
ورقة صالحة للأكل	edible paper
ورقة يمكن لعميل أو ضابط ابتلاعها لتجنّب فضح محتوياتها	paper that can be swallowed by an agent or officer to avoid its contents being compromised
إسقاط ميّت إلكترونيّ	electronic dead drop
تبادل معلومات إلكترونيّ بطريقة تخفي الرّابط بين المرسل والمستقبل	electronic exchange of information in a manner that obscures the link between the sender and receiver
تزيين	embellish
إضافة تفاصيل كاذبة إلى معلومات	to add false details to information
إنقاذ	exfiltration
إزالة فرد خلسةً من منطقة خاضعة لسيطرة عدوّ	clandestine removal of an individual from an area under enemy control
تصنيع	fabricate
ابتكار أو تضخيم معلومات	to invent or inflate information

نهج العلم المزيّف	false-flag approach
تصوير نفسه على أنّه مواطن من بلد آخر	representing oneself as a native of another country
تقرير معلومات ميدانيّ	field information report (FIR)
تقرير يقدّمه نشطاء ميدان	report filed by field operatives
حرج	flap
إحراج وتداعيات سياسيّة لعمليّة انكشفت	embarrassment and political repercussions of an exposed operation
إمكانيّة الإحراج	flap potential
احتماليّة الإحراج والتّداعيات السّياسيّة إذا انكشفت عمليّة	potential for embarrassment and political repercussions if an operation is exposed
جنيحات وأختام	flaps and seals
وحدة متخصّصة في فتح وثائق مختومة لاستغلال المعلومات الموجودة في تلك الوثائق دون ترك دليل على أنّها قد فُتِحت	unit specializing in opening sealed documents to exploit the information contained within the documents without leaving evidence that they have been opened

دفاع داخليّ أجنبيّ	foreign internal defense (FID)
إجراءات متَّخذة لتعزيز الدَفاع الدَاخليّ لحكومة أجنبيّة	actions taken to strengthen a foreign government's internal defense
اذهب بعيداً	go-away
إشارة إلى إحباط اتّصال معدٍّ له سلفاً	signal to abort a pre-arranged contact
اختبأ	go to ground
اختفاء عن الأنظار	to disappear into hiding
دعاية رماديّة	grey propaganda
دعاية لم يحدَّد مصدرها	propaganda whose source is not identi-fied
هدف صعب	hard target
فرد أو جماعة أو دولة أو نظام معادين يصعب اختراقهم	hostile individual, group, state or system that is difficult to pen-etrate
رفع الكعب	heel-lift
جهاز مستخدم ليسبّب عرجاً في مشية مرتديه من أجل تغيير مظهره	device used to cause the wearer to walk with a limp in order to change his/her appearance

بيئة معادية	hostile environment
بيئة خاضعة لسيطرة عدوّ	environment under enemy control
منطقة ساخنة	hot zone
منطقة خاضعة لتدابير أمنيّة مشدّدة	area under heightened security measures
تهديدات مختلطة	hybrid threats
تهديدات مؤلّفة من مجموعة تكتيكات وأساليب	threats comprised of a combination of tactics and methods
زرع	implant
جهاز إلكترونيّ مستخدم لاعتراض معلومات سرّاً	electronic device used to clandestinely inter-cept information
تسلّل	infiltrate
اختراق دولة أو منظّمة	to penetrate a country or organization
جاك في الصّندوق	jack-in-the-box
دمية بحجم رجل موضوعة كفخّ في سيّارة	man-sized dummy placed in an auto-mobile as a decoy
عمليّة مشتركة	joint operation
عمليّة أجرتها منظّمتين أو أكثر	operation conducted by two or more organi-zations

King George's cavalry

فرسان الملك جورج

British euphemism for paying someone off when all other options fail

كناية بريطانيّة عن دفع المال لشخص ما بعد فشل جميع الخيارات الأخرى

knuckle draggers

مفاصل ساحبة

euphemism for CIA paramilitary forces

كناية عن قوات وكالة الاستخبارات المركزيّة شبه العسكريّة

laundering

غسيل

transferring illegally obtained money through a third party to conceal its true source

تحويل أموال مكتسبة بشكل غير شرعيّ عن طريق طرف ثالث لإخفاء مصدرها الحقيقيَ

letter drop

مكان إسقاط رسالة

secret unattended location where an agent can leave something for pickup by his/her handler at a later time (*see also* dead drop)

مكان سرّيّ حيث يمكن لعميل ترك شيء ليلتقطه المسيّس في وقت لاحق (*أنظر إسقاط الميّت*)

live letterbox

صندوق الرّسائل الحيّة

address where mail is received for someone who does not live at that address

عنوان بريديّ لاستلام بريد لشخص لا يقيم في ذلك العنوان

تمرير	making a pass
تسليم رسالة إلى عنصر استخباراتيّ	handing a message to an intelligence operative
تصغير	microdot
نصّ مصغّر أو صور مصغّرة إلى حجم صغير جدّاً لتجنّب الكشف	text or images reduced to a very small size to avoid detection
عارٍ	naked
عمل دون غطاء	operating without cover
موقع مراقبة	observation post (OP)
منشأة مشرفة على هدف استخباراتيّ تُستخدَم لرصد الهدف	facility overlooking an intelligence target used for monitoring the target
مناخ العمل	operational climate
مناخ سياسيّ واقتصاديّ لبلد مستهدف	political and economic climate of a target country
استخبارات العمليّات	operational intelligence
استخبارات لازمة لدعم عمليّات سرّيّة	intelligence required to support clandestine operations

خطّة عمليّة	operational plan
خطّة تحدّد أهدافاً والوسائل اللّازمة لتحقيق تلك الأهداف	plan outlining objectives and the means of achieving them
أمن العمليّات	operational security (OPSEC)
تدابير لحماية سرّيّة المعلومات والعمليّات	measures to guard the secrecy of information and operations
استخدام تشغيليّ	operational use
استخدام فرد أو جماعة أو معلومات في عمليّة سرّيّة	the use of an individual, group or information in a clandestine operation
ضابط عمليّات	operations officer
ضابط يجنّد مصادر بشريّة ويشغّلها	officer who recruits and handles human sources
معلّب	packed up
يصف عمليّة استخباراتيّة منتهية	describes a terminated intelligence operation

مشروط	parole
تبادل شفهيّ محدّد مسبقاً يُستخدَم لتحديد عملاء استخباراتيّين آخرين (*أنظر إشارة تعرَّف*)	predetermined verbal exchange used to identify other intelligence operatives (*see also* recognition signal)
نمط	pattern
روتين يوميّ فريد من نوعه لفرد معيّن	daily routine unique to an individual
عمليّات اختراق	penetration operations
عمليّات تسلّل إلى منطقة من خلال إنسان أو وسائل إلكترونيّة	operations to infiltrate an area through human or electronic means
إعادة تشغيل	playback
إعادة بلد ثالث لعمليّة طبع معلومات زائفة زُرعت في إعلام بلد أجنبيّ	a third country's reprinting of false information planted in the media of a foreign country
دعاية	propaganda
معلومات كاذبة أو مخادعة تهدف إلى التأثير على حكومة أو جماعة أو كيان آخر	false or manipulative information designed to influence a government, group or other entity

شركة مملوكة	proprietary company
شركة خاصّة ظاهرياً تُستخدَم كغطاء لعمليّة استخباراتيّة	ostensibly private company used as cover for an intelligence operation
معلومات محميّة	protected information
معلومات يحصل عليها جهاز استخباراتيّ من مصدر سرّيّ	information an intelligence service obtains from a clandestine source
إثارة	provocation
نشاط يهدف إلى استفزاز منظّمة لتردّ بطريقة قد تسبّب بها الضّرر لنفسها	activity intended to provoke an organization to respond in a manner that will cause itself damage
إشارة تعرّف	recognition signal
تبادل لفظيّ محدّد سلفاً يُستخدَم لتحديد أفراد استخبارات آخرين (*أنظر مشروط*)	predetermined verbal exchange used to identify other intelligence operatives (*see also* parole)
التقاط عكسيّ بواسطة سيّارة	reverse car pick-up
التقاط حيث يقوم المصدر بالتقاط الضّابط	pick-up in which the source picks up the officer

تخريب	sabotage
إصابة النّاس أو الممتلكات عمداً لتحقيق هدف عسكريّ أو سياسيّ	willfully injuring people or property to achieve a military or political objective
بيت آمن	safe house
موقع آمن لدعم وإجراء عمليّات سرّيّة	secure facility for supporting or conducting clandestine operations
موقع الإشارة	signal site
موقع محدّد سلفاً حيث يضع ضابط علامةً للتّواصل مع ضابط آخر	prearranged location where an officer places a mark to communicate with another officer
توقيع	signature
خصائص مرتبطة بهدف ذي أهمّيّة مستخدمة للتّعرّف على أو تحديد مكان الهدف	characteristics associated with a target of interest used to identify or locate the target
هدف ناعم	soft target
هدف غير محميّ نسبيّاً	relatively unprotected target

شعبة الأنشطة الخاصّة	Special Activities Division (SAD)
فرع جهاز الاستخبارات الوطنيّة السَّرَيّة التَّابع لوكالة الاستخبارات المركزيّة والمكلَّف بتنفيذ عمليّات سرّيّة	branch of the CIA's National Clandestine Service (NCS) tasked with carrying out covert operations
متطلّبات التَّجميع الثَّابت	standing collection requirements
متطلّبات التَّجميع المستمرّ	ongoing collection requirements
محطّة	station
مركز العمليّات في الخارج	overseas operational center
إخفاء معلومات	steganography
طريقة إخفاء معلومات سرّيّة داخل نصّ عامّ أو صورة عامّة	method of concealing secret information within a public text or image
اندماج	submerge
الاختفاء عن الأنظار بعد الوصول إلى بلد أجنبيّ	to disappear from view after arriving in a foreign country
تخريب	subversion
إجراءات رامية لإضعاف حكومة	attempts to undermine a government

سطح	surface
الظُّهور بعد الاختباء	to reappear after having gone to ground
الدَّخول خلسةً	surreptitious entry
دخول إلى منشأة مستهدفة دون إجازة	entry into a target facility without a warrant
تطويق	surround
مراقبة هدف بشكل علنيّ دون إخفاء المراقبة	openly conducting surveillance of a target without concealing the surveillance
مراقبة	surveillance
مراقبة سرِّيّة لهدف	clandestine observation of a target
طريق كشف المراقبة	surveillance detection route
طريق متَّخذ لتحديد إذا ما كان فرد ما ملاحقاً	route taken to determine if an individual is being followed
استخبارات تكتيكيّة	tactical intelligence
استخبارات لازمة لدعم عمليّات تكتيكيّة	intelligence required to support tactical operations

هدف	target
أيّ فرد أو منطقة أو نظام أو كيان آخر توجّه ضدّه العمليّات	any individual, area, system or other entity against which operations are directed
قتل مستهدف	targeted killing
اغتيال شخص محدّد ومعيّن	the assassination of a specific, identified individual
استهداف	targeting
تحديد أهداف وترتيب أولويّاتها	identifying and prioritizing targets
حزمة الاستهداف	targeting package
حزمة تحتوي على معلومات أساسيّة حول هدف	package containing key information about a target
تكليف بمهامّ	tasking
تعيين مهمّة لفرد	assigning a task to an individual
إنهاء	terminate
إنهاء نشاط تشغيليَ	to end an operational activity

عمليّات بلد ثالث	third country operations
استخدام دولة أجنبيّة كمنصّة يمكن من خلالها جمع معلومات عن بلدان أخرى	using one foreign country as a platform from which to collect information about other countries
بيئة التّهديد	threat environment
مجموعة من التّهديدات تواجه كياناً	the combination of threats facing an entity
تهديدات	threats
قدرات ونوايا عدوّ	capabilities and intentions of an adversary
حرفيّة	tradecraft
تقنيات ومنهجيّات مستخدمة لإجراء عمليّات سرّيّة	techniques and methodologies used to conduct clandestine operations
سرّيّ	undercover
عمليّة تهدف إلى إخفاء وجود العمليّة أو كفيل العمليّة	operation designed to conceal the existence or sponsor of the operation

عمليّة أحادية الجانب	unilateral operation
عمليّة قائمة دون تنسيق مع جهاز استخباراتيَ أو حكومة البلد المستهدف	operation carried out with no coordination with the intelligence service or government of the target country
دعاية بيضاء	white propaganda
دعاية معروفة المصدر	propaganda whose source is declared

5. COUNTERINTELLIGENCE (CI)

accountable document control system	نظام التَحكّم بوثائق المساءلة
system to control classified information	نظام للتَحكّم بمعلومات مصنَّفة
active opposition	معارضة نشطة
counterintelligence service of a targeted adversary	جهاز استخبارات مكافحة التَجسّس لعدوَ مستهدف
adjudication	إصدار الحكم
evaluation of information collected during a security investigation to determine whether to grant or renew an individual's security clearance	تقييم معلومات جُمِعت خلال تحقيق أمنيّ لتحديد إمكانيّة منح تصريح أمنيَ لفرد أو تجديده

سرّيّ إداريّاً	administratively confidential
تسمية مستخدمة لمعلومات حسّاسة لأسباب إداريّة وليس لأسباب الأمن القوميّ	label used for information which is sensitive for administrative reasons rather than national security reasons
معلومات عكسيّة	adverse information
معلومات تعكس سلباً على قدرة فرد مرخّص له حماية معلومات مصنّفة	information that reflects poorly on a cleared individual's ability to safeguard classified information
عميل كيان أجنبيّ	agent of a foreign entity
فرد يشارك في تجسّس لحكومة أجنبيّة ولكن ليس موظّفاً لدى تلك الحكومة	individual who engages in espionage for a foreign government but who is not an employee of that government
مضادّ للعبث	anti-tamper
أنشطة هندسيّة النّظام لحماية التّكنولوجيا الهامّة	systems engineering activities to protect critical technology

أشخاص مصرّح لهم	authorized persons
أفراد مصرّح لهم الوصول إلى معلومات مصنّفة	individuals authorized to access classified information
مستتر	backdoor
برامج غير مصرّح بها مستخدمة لتجاوز ضوابط أمنيّة	unauthorized software used to bypass security controls
تحقيق في الخلفيّة	background investigation (BI)
تحقيق رسميّ في أنشطة فرد	official investigation of an individual's activities
ملفّ حسّاس	bigot case
عمليّة تحقيق حسّاسة والوصول إليها محظور على بعض الموظّفين	sensitive investigation with restricted personnel access
قائمة حسّاسة	bigot list
قائمة موظّفين مصرّح لهم بالوصول إلى معلومات حسّاسة	list of personnel authorized to access sensitive information

فخّ الكناري   canary trap

توزيع وثيقة مع اختلافات بسيطة على العديد من المستلمين لتحديد من يسرّب المعلومات   distribution of a document with minor discrepancies to multiple recipients to determine who leaks the information

تحذير   caveat

تعيين مستخدم غالباً بالتّنسيق مع تصنيف أمنيّ لتشديد القيود على توزيع الموادّ الحسّاسة   designation used, often in coordination with a security classification, to further restrict distribution of sensitive materials

شهادة تدمير   certificate of destruction

شهادة تؤكّد أنّ معلومات تمّ تدميرها على النّحو المطلوب   certificate verifying that information has been destroyed as required

سلسلة العهدة   chain of custody

طريقة تتتبّع حركة المعلومات المصنّفة   method of tracking the movement of classified information

classification   تصنيف

determination that information requires protection from disclosure; classifications are assigned based on the level of sensitivity and category of the information. Classification levels in the US include confidential, secret and top secret.   تحديد أنّ المعلومات تتطلّب حماية من الكشف؛ تعيَّن التّصنيفات على أساس مستوى حساسيّة المعلومات وفئتها. تشمل مستويات التّصنيف في الولايات المتّحدة معلومات محجوبة وسرّيَة وسرّيَة للغاية

classified information   معلومات مصنّفة

information that requires protection from disclosure   معلومات تتطلّب حماية من الكشف

Classified Information Procedures Act (CIPA)   قانون إجراءات المعلومات المصنّفة

a law allowing potentially classified information to be presented to a judge in private to determine if it may be used in open court   قانون يسمح بعرض معلومات قد تكون مصنّفة على قاض على انفراد لتحديد ما إذا كان ممكناً استخدامها في محكمة علنيّة

تصريح	clearance
تصريح للوصول إلى معلومات مصنّفة	authorization to access classified information
مصرّح له	cleared
يصف فرداً يمتلك تصريحاً للوصول إلى معلومات مصنّفة	describes an individual with authorization to access classified information
مقاول مصرّح له	cleared contractor (CC)
فرد يعمل لدى شركة مقاولات الحكومة ومخوّل للوصول إلى معلومات مصنّفة	individual employed by a government contracting company who is authorized to access classified information
مقاول مصرّح له التّعامل مع وزارة الدّفاع	cleared defense contractor (CDC)
شركة مصرّح لها الوصول إلى معلومات مصنّفة	company authorized to access classified information
محفوظ بسرّية	close held
مشروع حسّاس للغاية يحتاج إلى ترخيص عالي المستوى للوصول إلى المعلومات	highly sensitive project with only high-level access to information

تقسيم	compartmentation
تقييد الوصول إلى معلومات حسّاسة إلّا لأفراد أو إدارات عندهم «الحاجة إلى المعرفة»	limiting access to sensitive information to those individuals or departments with a "need-to-know"
تحقيق بسبب شكوى	complaint-type investigation
تحقيق استخبارات مضادّة ناتج عن اشتباه في التّجسّس أوالتّخريب أو أعمال أخرى ارتُكبت عمداً ضدّ الدّولة أو جهاز الاستخبارات	counterintelligence investigation resulting from suspected espionage, sabotage or other acts wilfully committed against the state or intelligence service
مفضوح	compromised
وصول إليها من قبل أفراد غير مرخّص لهم	accessed by unauthorized individuals
خصوصيّ أو سرّيّ	confidential
تصنيف ينطبق على معلومات قد يؤدّي الكشف عنها إلى أضرار في الأمن القوميّ	classification applied to information whose disclosure could cause damage to national security

تلوّث | contamination

إدخال معلومات مصنّفة إلى جهاز كمبيوتر أو عرضها على متلقٍ يفتقر إلى مستوى التّصريح اللّازم للوصول إلى تلك المعلومات | the introduction of classified information to a computer or recipient lacking the clearance level required to access that information

تقييم مستمرّ | continuous evaluation

مراجعة مستمرّة لفرد يمتلك تصريحاً أمنيّاً لضمان أنّه لا يزال يلبّي متطلّبات التّصريح الأمنيّ | continually reviewing an individual with a security clearance to ensure he or she continues to meet the requirements for the security clearance

معلومات خاضعة للسّيطرة | controlled information

تمرير معلومات لعدوّ عن قصد لإثارة استجابة مطلوبة | information intentionally passed to an adversary to provoke a desired response

معلومات غير مصنّفة خاضعة للسّيطرة	controlled unclassified information
معلومات لا تلبّي معيار التّصنيف السّرّيّ ولكنّها مع ذلك يجب أن تكون محميّة من الكشف	information which does not meet the standard for classification but which must nevertheless be protected from disclosure
مطبوخ	cooked
مزيج من موادّ حقيقيّة ووهميّة	comprised of a mixture of genuine and fake material
مكافحة الخداع	counterdeception
جهود رامية إلى إبطال أو استغلال عمليّات الخداع من عدوّ	efforts to neutralize or exploit an adversary's deception operations
مكافحة التّجسّس	counterespionage
جهود لمنع أو إبطال أو استغلال أنشطة تجسّس عدوّ	efforts to prevent, neutralize or exploit an adversary's espionage activities
استخبارات مضادّة	counterintelligence (CI)
جهود لتحديد وإبطال ومكافحة واستغلال أنشطة تجسّس عدوّ	efforts to identify, neutralize, counter and exploit an adversary's espionage activities

counterintelligence analysis	تحليل الاستخبارات المضادّة
analysis of the capabilities and intentions of foreign intelligence agencies or sub-state actors	تحليل قدرات ونوايا وكالات استخباراتيّة أجنبيّة أو جهات غير حكوميّة
counterintelligence appraisal	تقدير الاستخبارات المضادّة
appraisal of an adversary's capabilities	تقييم قدرات عدوّ
counterintelligence assessment	تقييم الاستخبارات المضادّة
report outlining the findings of counterintelligence analysis	تقرير يوجز نتائج تحليل مكافحة التَّجسّس
counterintelligence awareness	وعي الاستخبارات المضادّة
awareness of the sensitivity of information, the potential threats to sensitive information and appropriate responses to perceived threats to sensitive information	إدراك مدى حساسيّة معلومات والتَّهديدات المحتملة لمعلومات حسّاسة والاستجابات المناسبة للتَّهديدات المتصوّرة لمعلومات حسّاسة
counterintelligence collection	تجميع الاستخبارات المضادّة

جهود للحصول على معلومات متعلّقة بأنشطة استخباراتيّة أجرتها حكومات أجنبيّة أو جهات غير حكوميّة	efforts to acquire information regarding intelligence activities conducted by foreign governments or sub-state actors
رايات الاستخبارات المضادّة	counterintelligence flags
مؤشّرات تدلّ على أنّ مصدراً قد لا يكون جديراً بالثّقة	indicators that a source may not be trustworthy
تفتيش الاستخبارات المضادّة	counterintelligence inspection
تفتيش لتحديد مدى الالتزام بسياسات وإجراءات معمول بها	inspection to determine adherence to applicable policies and procedures
تحقيق الاستخبارات المضادّة	counterintelligence investigation
جهود لتحديد ما إذا كان فرد يتصرَف نيابة عن حكومة أجنبيّة أو مجموعة غير حكوميّة	efforts to determine if an individual is acting on behalf of a foreign government or sub-state actor

عمليّات الاستخبارات المضادّة counterintelligence operations

أنشطة تُنفَّذ لعرقلة أو استغلال أنشطة استخبارات حكومة أجنبيّة أو مجموعة غير حكوميّة activities undertaken to hinder or exploit the intelligence activities of a foreign government or sub-state actor

جهاز كشف الكذب للاستخبارات المضادّة counterintelligence scope polygraph (CI scope poly)

استجواب بواسطة جهاز كشف الكذب لتحديد ما إذا كان فرد ينتمي إلى أو يتصرّف نيابة عن حكومة أجنبيّة أو مجموعة غير حكوميّة polygraph examination to determine whether or not an individual is affiliated with or acting on behalf of a foreign government or sub-state actor

تسريب مضادّ counterleak

تسريب متعمّد لمعلومات أو تضليل لمواجهة تسريب سابق intentional leak of information or disinformation to counter a previous leak

تدابير مضادّة countermeasures

تدابير متّخذة لمنع فاعليّة عمليّات عدوّ measures taken to inhibit an adversary's operational effectiveness

مكافحة التَّخريب	countersabotage
جهود لإضعاف أو تدمير قدرة عدوَ على القيام بأنشطة تخريبيَّة	efforts to degrade or destroy an adversary's ability to conduct sabotage activities
تجسّس مضادّ	counterspy
وضع جاسوس داخل مؤسَسة عدوَ	spy placed within an adversary's organization
مكافحة التَّقويض	countersubversion
جهود لإضعاف أو تدمير قدرة عدوَ على إجراء أنشطة تقويض	efforts to degrade or destroy an adversary's ability to conduct subversion activities
مكافحة المراقبة	countersurveillance
تدابير لمنع المراقبة	measures to prevent surveillance
معلومات هامَة	critical information
معلومات حسَّاسة قد يؤدّي انكشافها إلى تمكّن خصوم من منع نجاح مهمَّة	sensitive information which, if disclosed, could enable adversaries to prevent the success of a mission

custodian حارس

individual responsible for a piece or pieces of classified information فرد مسؤول عن جزء أو أجزاء من معلومات مصنّفة

damage assessment تقييم الضّرر

assessment of the impact of disclosed classified information تقييم آثار انكشاف معلومات مصنّفة

dangle تلويح

asset intentionally placed to tempt a rival intelligence agency to recruit the asset مصدر موجّه وُضِع عمداً لإغراء وكالة استخباراتيّة منافسة لتجنّده

deception خداع

measures to mislead an adversary تدابير رامية إلى تضليل عدوّ

declassification رفع حكم السّرّيّة

changing the status of information from classified to unclassified تغيير وضع معلومات من مصنّف إلى غير مصنّف

أنشطة دفاعيّة لاستخبارات مضادّة	defensive counterintelli-gence activities
أنشطة استخباراتيّة مضادّة تهدف إلى حماية معلومات وأفراد من الاستغلال من قبل أعداء	counterintelligence activities aimed at protecting infor-mation and personnel against exploitation by adversaries
فضح متعمّد	deliberate compromise
نشر معلومات مصنّفة أو سوء استعمالها عمداً	intentionally dissemi-nating or misusing classified information
إنكار	denial
جهود لإخفاء معلومات حسّاسة وحمايتها من تجميع استخبارات أجنبيّة لها	efforts to conceal sensi-tive information and protect it from for-eign intelligence collection
إنكار وخداع	denial and deception
الإنكار يُستخدَم لإخفاء الحقيقة	denial is used to hide the truth
الخداع يُستخدَم لتصوير معلومات كاذبة على أنّها صحيحة	deception is used to portray false infor-mation as true

تصنيف مشتقّ	derivative classification
تحديد أنّ موادّاً تحتوي على معلومات تمّ تصنيفها سرّاً في مكان آخر	determination that material contains information that has been classified else-where
إدراك مطلوب	desired perception
معلومات كاذبة يجب أن يؤمن بها هدف لإنجاح عمليّة	false information a tar-get must believe for an operation to be successful
إجراءات التّدمير	destruction procedures
إجراءات لتدمير موادّ	procedures for destroy-ing materials
تضليل	disinformation
معلومات كاذبة تهدف إلى خداع فرد أو جماعة أو حكومة أجنبيّة	false information aimed at deceiving an indi-vidual, group, or foreign government
عميل مزدوج	double agent
فرد يعمل لصالح جهاز استخباراتيّ بينما يخضع لسيطرة حكومة أخرى سرّاً	individual working for an intelligence ser-vice while secretly under the control of another government

مضاعف doubled

يصف عميلاً تحت سيطرة describes an agent un-
وكالة استخباراتيّة أجنبيّة der the control of a
يقوم بتوفير معلومات زائفة foreign intelligence
لوكالة الاستخبارات الخاصّة agency who provides
به fake information to
his own intelligence
service

تخفيض التّصنيف downgrade

خفض مستوى التصنيف to reduce the classifica-
السّرّيّ للموادّ tion level of material

آذان فقط ears only

رمز يشير إلى معلومات من code indicating infor-
الممنوع كتابتها mation that may not
be written down

عيون فقط eyes only

مخصّص لعيون أشخاص intended only for the
مكلّفين فقط eyes of designated
individuals

تصريح المنشأة facility clearance

تحديد أنّ خزين معلومات determination that clas-
مصنّفة مسموح به في sified information
منشأة معيّنة may be stored in a
given facility

تأكيد زائف	false confirmation
عمليّة خداع لجعل تضليل مقدّم لعدوٍّ يظهر وكأنّه ذو مصداقيّة	deception operation to make disinformation provided to an adversary appear credible
تعليقات	feedback
تقرير بشأن التّقدّم المحرز في عمليّة استخباراتيّة مضادّة	report regarding the progress of a counterintelligence operation
أنشطة الاستخبارات المضادّة على نطاق واسع	full-spectrum counterintelligence activities
مجموعة كاملة من أنشطة استخباراتيّة مضادّة يمكن لجهاز استخدامها لتحقيق أهدافه	full range of counterintelligence activities that a service can use to achieve its aims
وصل	hand receipt
وثيقة تسجيل استلام فرد للموادّ	document recording an individual's receipt of material
كشف غير مقصود	inadvertent disclosure
كشف عرضيّ لمعلومات مصنّفة	accidental disclosure of classified information

أمن صناعيّ	industrial security
تنفيذ تدابير لحماية معلومات مصنّفة تستخدمها شركات خاصّة عاملة بموجب عقود حكوميّة	implementation of measures to protect classified information accessed by private companies working on government contracts
تأمين المعلومات	information assurance
تدابير لحماية معلومات	measures to protect information
أمن المعلومات	information security
تدابير لحماية معلومات من الوصول إلى غير المصرّح لهم مع ضمان استمراريّة وصولها إلى المستخدمين المخوّلين	measures to protect information from unauthorized access and ensure its continued access to authorized users
تسريب	leak
انكشاف معلومات مصنّفة، سواءً كان الكشف متعمّداً أو عرضيّاً	disclosure of classified information, whether intentional or accidental

litmus test	اختبار المصداقيّة
counterintelligence operation whereby false information is provided to a suspected informant to monitor what he or she does with that false information	عمليّة استخباراتيّة مضادّة حيث تُقدَّم معلومات كاذبة إلى مخبر لمراقبة كيف يستخدم تلك المعلومات الكاذبة
manipulation	تلاعب
combination of true and false information to deceive an adversary	جمع بين معلومات صحيحة وكاذبة لخداع عدوّ
marking	تعليم \ تأشير
adding security classifications to classified material	إضافة تصنيفات أمنيّة إلى موادّ مصنّفة
misdirection	تضليل
efforts to divert the attention of an adversary or other entity from an operation, individual, or information	جهود لتحويل انتباه عدوّ أو كيان آخر عن عمليّة أو فرد أو معلومات

mole مخبر أو عميل

individual engaged in espionage against an intelligence service from within that service فرد مشترك في تجسّس ضدّ جهاز استخباراتيّ من داخل هذا الجهاز

mole hunt بحث عن عميل

search for moles within a service بحث عن عملاء داخل وكالة

need-to-know حاجة إلى المعرفة

determination that an individual requires access to information تحديد أنّ فرداً يتطلّب الوصول إلى معلومات

no foreign distribution (NOFORN) ممنوع التّوزيع الأجنبيّ

distribution code prohibiting the distribution of infor-mation to foreign entities رمز توزيع يمنع توزيع معلومات لكيانات أجنبيّة

nothing recorded against (NRA) لا شيء مسجّل ضدّه

British term for an indi-vidual against whom no derogatory infor-mation is discovered during a security investigation مصطلح بريطانيّ لفرد لم يتمّ اكتشاف أيّة معلومات ضدّه خلال تحقيق أمنيّ

أنشطة استخبارات مضادّة	offensive counterintelli-gence activities
أنشطة استخباراتيّة مضادّة تهدف إلى اختراق جهاز استخباراتيّ عدوّ	counterintelligence activities aimed at penetrating an adver-sary's intelligence service
عميل الاختراق	penetration agent
عميل مزروع في جهاز استخباراتيّ أجنبيّ لرصد نجاحات وإخفاقات عمليّات الاستخباراتيّة المضادّة	agent planted in a for-eign intelligence service to monitor the successes and failures of his/her service's counterintelligence operations
موادّ اللّعب	play material
معلومات مفصح عنها عمداً لصالح وكالة أجنبيّة لتأسيس مصداقيّة عميل متسلّل	information deliberately disclosed to a foreign service to establish the credibility of an infiltration agent
أمن وقائيّ	protective security
مصطلح بريطانيّ لحماية معلومات مصنّفة	British term for the pro-tection of classified information

شائعة	rumor
تضليل معقول يُنشَر لإيذاء عدوّ	plausible disinformation disseminated to harm an adversary
حيلة	ruse
خدعة للاحتيال على عدوّ وغالباً من خلال تعريض عدوّ إلى التَّضليل	trick to deceive an adversary, often by exposing an adversary to disinformation
سرّيّ	secret
تصنيف ينطبق على معلومات قد يؤدّي انكشافها إلى أضرار جسيمة بالأمن القوميّ	classification applied to information whose disclosure could cause serious damage to national security
حسّاس	sensitive
معلومات تتطلّب الحماية من الانكشاف	information requiring protection from disclosure
مرفق المعلومات المقسَّمة الحسّاسة	sensitive compartmented information facility (SCIF)
منشأة مصمَّمة للتّعامل والتّخزين الآمن لمعلومات مصنَّفة	facility designed for the secure handling and storage of classified information
حماية المصدر	source protection

عبارة تُستَخدم في بداية مراسلة لتشير إلى أنَّ محتوياتها تتطلّب الحماية الوثيقة	phrase used at the beginning of a communication indicating that its contents must be closely protected
إنهاء خدمة	takedown
تدمير شبكة استخباراتيّة معادية	the destruction of a hostile intelligence network
سرّيّ للغاية	top secret
تصنيف ينطبق على معلومات قد يؤدّي انكشافها إلى أضرار فادحة في الأمن القوميّ	classification applied to information whose disclosure could cause very grave damage to national security
ترقية	upgrade
زيادة مستوى تصنيف الموادّ	to heighten the classification level of material

6. SIGNALS INTELLIGENCE (SIGINT)

استخبارات صوتيّة	acoustic intelligence (ACINT)
تجميع ومعالجة معلومات مستمدّة من أصوات	collection and processing of information derived from sounds
أمن صوتيّ	acoustical security
تدابير لمنع أفراد غير مصرّح لهم من سماع معلومات مصنّفة	measures to prevent unauthorized individuals from hearing classified information
مراقبة صوتيّة	acoustical surveillance
استخدام أجهزة إلكترونيّة لجمع معلومات صادرة عن أصوات	the use of electronic devices to collect information derived from sounds
بيانات مؤرشفة	archived data
بيانات مخزّنة في مستودع	data stored in a repository
مصادقة	authentication
نظام أمنيّ لمصادقة الإرسال	security system to authenticate transmissions

botnet   بوتنيت

robot network; a net-   شبكة الرّوبوت؛ شبكة من
work of computers   أجهزة كمبيوتر يتحكّم بها
controlled by one   فرد أو مجموعة معيّنة
individual or group

brevity code   رمز الإيجاز

code used to shorten a   رمز مستخدم لتقصير رسالة
message but not to   ولكن ليس لحجب محتوياتها
obscure its contents

bulk collection   تجميع بكمّيّات كبيرة

indiscriminate collec-   تجميع عشوائيّ لكمّيّات كبيرة
tion of large   من البيانات
quantities of data

case notation   تدوين حالة

letters or numbers used   حروف أو أرقام مستخدمة
to identify a network   لتحديد اعتراض شبكة
interception

cipher   تشفير

information written in   معلومات مكتوبة برموز لإخفاء
code to conceal its   معناها الحقيقيّ
true meaning

اصطياد النّاقر	click-jacking
إخفاء روابط تشعّبيّة ضارّة تحت روابط مشروعة ليقوم المستخدمون بالنّقر عليها دون قصد	hiding malicious hyper-links beneath legitimate links to cause users to unwit-tingly click on them
تجميع بواسطة وصول عن قرب	close access collection
تجميع انبثاقات غير مقصودة من أجهزة الكمبيوتر	collection of uninten-tional emanations from computer equip-ment
كتاب الرّموز	code book
وثيقة تحدّد الرّمز وما يقابله من نصّ عادٍ من دون رموز	document outlining the code and its corres-ponding plain text
غرفة الرّموز	code room
منشأة حيث يتمّ التّرميز والتّشفير	facility in which coding and ciphering take place
كلمة رمز	code word
كلمة ذات معنى محدّد سلفاً مختلف من تعريفها في القاموس	word with a predeter-mined meaning outside of its diction-ary definition

تحليل الاتّصالات	communications analysis
تحليل معلومات استخباراتيّة جُمِعت من خلال اعتراض الاتّصالات	analysis of intelligence gathered through the interception of communications
غطاء الاتّصالات	communications cover
جهود لإخفاء رسائل عن عدوّ	efforts to conceal communications from an adversary
استخبارات الاتّصالات	communications intelligence (COMINT)
معلومات استخباراتيّة مجمّعة من خلال اعتراض الاتّصالات	intelligence gathered through the interception of communications
أمن الاتّصالات	communications security (COMSEC)
تدابير لحماية الاتّصالات	measures to protect communications
تحليل أمن الاتّصالات	communications security analysis
تحليل أمن الاتّصالات وأنظمتها	analysis of the security of communications and communications systems

رصد أمن الاتّصالات communications security monitoring

مراقبة الفرد لنظام الاتّصالات الخاصّ به لتقييم أمن النّظام monitoring one's own communications system to assess the security of the system

مراقبة أمن الاتّصالات communications security surveillance

رصد اتّصالات لتحديد مستوى أمن الاتّصالات وتحديد نقاط الضّعف الأمنيّة monitoring of communications to determine the level of communications security and to identify security vulnerabilities

هجوم على شبكة الحاسوب computer network attack (CNA)

عمليّة لتخفيض كفاءة حواسيب أو شبكات أو تدميرها operation to degrade or destroy computers or networks

دفاع شبكة الحاسوب computer network defense (CND)

جهود لحماية شبكات الحاسوب من الهجمات efforts to protect computer networks against attacks

استغلال شبكة الحاسوب	computer network exploitation (CNE)
عمليّة استخراج معلومات من حواسيب أو شبكات	operation to extract information from computers or networks
أمن الحاسوب	computer security (COMPUSEC)
حماية ضدّ الدّخول غير المصرّح به و/أو ضدّ استغلال الحواسيب	protection against unauthorized access and/or exploitation of computers
متعدٍّ على جهاز حاسوب	computer trespasser
فرد يصل إلى جهاز حاسوب آمن وهو غير مصرّح له	unauthorized individual who accesses a secure computer
مراقبة إلكترونيّة توافقيّة	consensual electronic surveillance
رصد طرف قد وافق على أن تتمّ مراقبته	monitoring a party which has consented to be monitored
تسلسل الاتّصالات	contact chaining
استخدام اللّوغاريتمات لتحديد سلسلة ارتباطات شخص ذي فائدة	the use of algorithms to identify a person of interest's chain of connections

corporate partner access	الاختراق بالتَّعاون المشترك
cooperation with corporations to access communications systems	تعاون مع شركات للوصول إلى أنظمة اتّصالات
cover term	مصطلح غطاء
a program's codename	اسم رمزيّ لبرنامج
cryptanalysis	تحليل الشَفرات
breaking codes or ciphers	كسر رموز أو شفرات
cryptocommunication	تشفير الاتّصالات
encrypted communications	اتّصالات مشفَّرة
cryptogram	برقيّة مشفَّرة
encoded text	نصّ مشفَّر
cryptographer	مشفَّر
individual who encrypts or decrypts communications	فرد يشفَّر أو يفكّ شفرة اتّصالات
cryptography	كتابة مشفَّرة
writing codes or ciphers	كتابة رموز أو شفرات

مركز التّشفير	cryptologic center
مركز إقليميّ لاستخبارات الإشارات	regional SIGINT center
علم التّشفير	cryptology
دراسة التّشفير وتحليل الشّفرات	the study of cryptography and cryptanalysis
موادّ التّشفير	cryptomaterial
جميع الموادّ المستخدمة في التّشفير	all materials used for cryptography
اسم رمزيّ	cryptonym
رمز مخصّص لفرد من أجل طمس هويّته في الاتّصالات	code name assigned to an individual in order to obscure his/her identification in communications
أمن التّشفير	cryptosecurity
تدابير لحماية أنظمة تشفير من الاعتراض وفكّ التّشفير والاكتشاف والعبث	measures to protect encryption systems from interception, decryption, discovery and tampering
نظام تشفير	cryptosystem
نظام كتابة رموز أو شفرات	system of writing codes or ciphers

cuts عيّنات

excerpts of conversa-
tions collected by
SIGINT operations
مقتطفات من محادثات جمعتها
عمليّات استخبارات
الإشارات

cyber espionage تجسّس حاسوبيّ

exploitation of
computers and/or
computer networks to
obtain secrets
استغلال حواسيب و/أو شبكات
الحاسوب للحصول على
أسرار

cyber incident حادث حاسوبيّ

actual or attempted in-
trusion into a
computer system or
network
اقتحام فعليّ أو محاولة اقتحام
نظام حاسوب أو شبكة

cyberterrorism إرهاب حاسوبيّ

the use of computers
and information tech-
nology systems to
cause damage or de-
struction to further a
political objective
استخدام الحواسيب وأنظمة
تكنولوجيا المعلومات
لإحداث ضرر أو دمار
لتعزيز هدف سياسيّ

data mining تنقيب عن معلومات

extracting information
and patterns from
large sets of data
استخراج معلومات وأنماط من
مجموعات كبيرة من
البيانات

فكّ الشّفرة	decipher
تحويل نصّ مشفّر إلى نصّ عادٍ باستخدام نظام تشفير	to convert an enciphered text into plain text using a cipher system
حلّ رموز الشّفرة	decode
تحويل رمز إلى نصّ عادٍ باستخدام نظام تشفير	to convert code into plain text using a code system
فكّ التّشفير	decrypt
تحويل نصّ مشفّر إلى نصّ عادٍ باستخدام نظام تشفير	to convert encrypted text into plain text using a cryptosystem
غوص عميق	deep dive
نظام تجميع يمكن من خلاله تجميع كمّيّات كبيرة من المعلومات عن سلوك مستخدم في فترة قصيرة من الزّمن	collection system which enables the collection of large amounts of information on user behavior in a short period of time
حرفيّة رقميّة	digital tradecraft
طرق استخدام الإنترنت والقدرات الرّقميّة للتّجسّس	methods of employing cyber and digital capabilities for espionage

تعيين الاتِّجاه	direction finding (DF)
عمليّة مستخدمة لتحديد موقع جهاز إرسال	process used to pinpoint the position of a transmitter
قاعدة بيانات موزّعة	distributed database
قاعدة بيانات المعلومات المقسَّمة والمخزّنة على حواسيب مختلفة	database of information which is compartmented and stored on different computers
معالجة موزّعة	distributed processing
استخدام حواسيب متعدّدة لمعالجة بيانات	using multiple computers to process data
نظام موزّع	distributed system
نظام حواسيب متَّصلة تتقاسم مهامّاً موكَّلة إلى النّظام	system of interconnected computers which share tasks assigned to the system
فهرس المراقبة الإلكترونيّة	electronic surveillance (ELSUR) index
قائمة الأفراد الَّذين خضعوا لمراقبة مكتب التَّحقيقات الفيدراليَ	list of individuals who have been under Federal Bureau of Investigation (FBI) surveillance

كهرومغناطيسيّ	electromagnetic (EM)
متعلّق بالكهرومغناطيسيّة	relating to electromagnetism
تدابير إلكترونيّة مضادّة	electronic countermeasures
جهود لتقييد استخدام عدوّ لأنظمة الاتّصالات	efforts to restrict an adversary's use of communications systems
خداع إلكترونيّ	electronic deception
استخدام أنظمة اتّصالات لخداع عدوّ	use of communications systems to deceive an adversary
استخبارات إلكترونيّة	electronic intelligence (ELINT)
استخبارات مستمدّة من باعثي الاتّصالات	intelligence derived from communications emitters
حرب إلكترونيّة	electronic warfare
إجراءات متّخذة للسّيطرة على الطّيف الكهرومغناطيسيّ	actions taken to control the electromagnetic spectrum

تدابير الحرب الإلكترونيّة المساندة	electronic warfare support measures (ESM)
جهود لتحديد هويّة مصادر الطّاقة الكهرومغناطيسيّة ومكانها لغرض الكشف عن التّهديد	efforts to identify and locate sources of electromagnetic energy for the purpose of threat detection
تشفير سايفر	encipher
تحويل نصّ عادٍ إلى رمز باستخدام نظام تشفير	to convert plain text into code using a cipher system
ترميز أو تشفير	encode
تحويل نصّ عادٍ إلى رمز باستخدام نظام تشفير	to convert plain text into code using a code system
شفّر	encrypt
تحويل نصّ عادٍ إلى رمز باستخدام نظام تشفير	to convert plain text into code using a cryptosystem
استغلال	exploitation
تجميع واستخدام معلومات استخباراتيّة	collection and use of intelligence information

جدار حماية	firewall
نظام مصمّم لضبط الدّخول بين شبكات وأنظمة الحاسوب	system designed to limit access between computer networks and systems
اختراق خارجيّ لجهاز حاسوب	foreign computer intrusion
محاولة تسلّل أو تسلّل فعليّ إلى نظام حاسوب مصنّف من قبل أو نيابة عن كيان أجنبيّ	attempted or actual intrusion into a classified computer system by or on behalf of a foreign entity
قانون مراقبة الاستخبارات الأجنبيّة	Foreign Intelligence Surveillance Act (FISA)
سلطة وتوجيهات قانونيّة للمراقبة والتّفتيش من قبل أجهزة استخبارات الولايات المتّحدة داخل الولايات المتّحدة لتجميع معلومات استخباراتيّة أجنبيّة	legal authority and guidelines for surveillance and searches by US intelligence services within the US for the purpose of foreign intelligence collection
بخّر	fumigate
تدابير لكشف أجهزة تنصّت إلكترونيّة مخبّأة وتعطيلها	measures to detect and neutralize concealed electronic listening devices

قرصان حاسوب   hacker

فرد يحاول الالتفاف على نظام
أمن حاسوب ليحقّق دخولاً
غير مصرّح به   individual who attempts to circumvent a computer's security system to gain unauthorized access

جانب عالٍ   high side

نظام حاسوبيّ مصنّف   classified computer system

لفظة متجانسة   homophone

نظام تشفير يستخدم بدائل عن
حروف   cryptographic system using substitutes for letters

وعاء عسل   honey pot

فخّ مصمّم لجذب متسلّلين
محتملين إلى نظم معلومات   trap designed to attract potential intruders into information systems

هوف داف   huff duff

عبارة «عثورٍ على اتّجاه عالي
التّردّد» باللّغة العاميّة   slang for "high frequency direction finding" (HF/DF)

التّضليل بتزييف اتّصالات	imitative communication deception (ICD)
إدخال اتّصالات كاذبة تشبه اتّصالات مشروعة إلى نظام اتّصالات عدوّ	introducing false communications, resembling legitimate communications, into an adversary's communications system
تجميع غير مقصود	inadvertent collection
استهداف غير مشروع و غير متعمّد لمواطن أمريكيّ في الولايات المتّحدة	in the US, unintentional illegal targeting of a US citizen
تجميع عرضيّ	incidental collection
معلومات عن مواطن أمريكيّ تمّ الحصول عليها بشكل عرضيّ أثناء عمليّات استهدفت مواطناً أجانبيّاً في الولايات المتّحدة	in the US, information about a US citizen incidentally obtained during the course of operations targeting a foreign national
مؤشّر	indicator
عنصر داخل نصّ مشفّر يوجّه لفكّ تشفير	element within an encrypted text which guides decryption

intercept اعتراض

clandestine capture of signals without the consent of the emitter or intended recipient of the signals

التقاط إشارات سرّاً دون موافقة الباعث أو متلقّي الإشارات المقصود

interdiction اعتراض أجهزة

SIGINT operation in which electronics equipment is intercepted in order to plant monitoring devices on the equipment before redirecting it to its destination

عمليّات استخبارات الإشارات الّتي يتمّ فيها اعتراض المعدّات الإلكترونيّة من أجل زرع أجهزة مراقبة على المعدّات قبل إعادة توجيهها إلى مقصدها

intrusion تطفّل

unauthorized entry into an information system

دخول غير مصرّح به إلى نظام معلومات

jamming تشويش

actions to deny an adversary's use of communications systems

إجراءات لمنع استخدام عدوّ لأنظمة اتّصالات

مفتاح	key
رمز مستخدم لتشفير نصّ عادٍ أو فكّ تشفير نصّ مشفّر	code used to encrypt plain text or decrypt encrypted text
مولّد مفتاح	key generator
برنامج حاسوب مستخدم لتوليد مفتاح ترخيص المنتج بشكل شرعيّ أو غير شرعيّ	computer program used to generate a product licensing key legiti- mately or illegitimately
محطّة تنصّت	listening post
محطّة على مقربة من هدف مستخدمة لاعتراض الاتّصالات الخاصّة بالهدف	station in close proxim- ity to a target used to intercept the target's communications
استراق السّمع المباشر	live tap
تنصّت هاتفيّ يراقبه فرد في الوقت الفوريّ بدلاً عن التّسجيل	telephonic tap which is monitored by an indi- vidual in real time rather than recorded
جانب منخفض	low side
نظام حاسوب غير مصنّف	unclassified computer system

خداع إلكترونيّ للتّلاعب	manipulative electronic deception
جهود لتضليل عدوّ وإخفاء أنشطة باستخدام أجهزة استشعار و/أو راديو	efforts to mislead an adversary and conceal activities using sensor and/or radio equipment
بيانات وصفيّة	metadata
معلومات يتمّ جمعها عن الاتّصالات، مثل التّوجيه أو تأشير المعلومات، ولكنّها تستثني المحتوى الفعليّ للرّسائل	information which is collected about communications, such as routing or signaling information, but which excludes the actual content of the communications
رصد	monitor
مراقبة اتّصالات إلكترونيّة	observation of electronic communications
تشفير أحاديّ الأبجديّة	monoalphabetic cipher
تشفير يستخدم بدائل مفردة للحروف الأبجديّة	cipher using a single substitution alphabet
وكالة الأمن القوميّ	National Security Agency (NSA)
وكالة أمريكيّة مسؤولة عن استخبارات الإشارات	US agency responsible for signals intelligence (SIGINT)

وسادة لمرّة واحدة	one-time pad
تقنيّة تشفير حيث يُستخدَم رمز مرة واحدة فقط لمنع كسر الرّمز	encryption technique whereby a code is used only one time to prevent code-breaking
نصّ مفتوح	open text
رسالة غير مشفَرة	message which is not encoded
تجميع من فوق	overhead collection
استخدام أشياء فوق سطح الأرض، مثل طائرات دون طيّار أو أقمار اصطناعيّة، لجمع بيانات	the use of objects above the earth's surface, such as drones or satellites, to collect data
تشفير متعدّد الأبجديّة	polyalphabetic cipher
تشفير يستخدم بدائل متعدّدة لأحرف الأبجديّة	cipher using multiple substitution alphabets
بريزم	Prism
برنامج وكالة الأمن القوميّ يهدف إلى جمع معلومات الاتّصالات من شركات التّكنولوجيا	NSA program aimed at collecting communications information from technology companies

تنقيح redaction

إزالة أو تسويد كلمات أو
أجزاء من وثيقة بحيث
يستمرّ تصنيفها السّرّيّ
عندما تُرفع السّرّيّة عن
الوثيقة نفسها
removing or blacking
out words or sections
of a document which
remain classified
when the document
itself is declassified

هاتف آمن secure telephone

هاتف مجهّز لمنع رصد
المحادثات
telephone equipped to
prevent the monitor-
ing of conversations

مستشعر sensor

جهاز مبرمج لكشف منبّه device programmed to
detect a stimulus

استخبارات الإشارات signals intelligence
(SIGINT)

تجميع معلومات استخباراتيّة
من خلال اعتراض إشارات؛
ويشمل الاستخبارات
الإلكترونيّة واستخبارات
الاتّصالات
collection of intelli-
gence through signals
interception; includes
electronic intelligence
(ELINT) and commu-
nications intelligence
(COMINT)

أمن الإشارات signals security
(SIGSEC)

أمن الاتّصالات والإكترونيّات communications and
electronics security

هاتف معقّم   sterile telephone

هاتف لا يمكن تعقّب موقعه   telephone whose location is untraceable

بيانات وصفيّة لاتّصالات هاتفيّة   telephony metadata

معلومات يتمّ جمعها عن اتّصالات هاتفيّة إلّا أنّها لا تشمل مضمون الاتّصالات   information which is collected about telephonic communications but which excludes the content of the communications

اعتراض نصوص   text interception

اعتراض اتّصالات نصّيّة   interception of textual communications

استخبارات إشارات أجهزة أجنبيّة   foreign instrumentation signals intelligence (FISINT)

فرع من الاستخبارات الإلكترونيّة، معلومات استخباراتيّة مستمدّة من اعتراض بيانات من أنظمة مراقبة عن بعد   subset of ELINT, intelligence derived from the interception of data from remotely monitored systems

تحليل المرور   traffic analysis

تحليل اتّصالات لتحديد الأنماط   analysis of communications to identify patterns

تجميع فوقيّ	upstream collection
تجميع محتوى الاتّصالات وبياناتها الوصفيّة أثناء مرورها من خلال البنية التّحتيّة للاتّصالات	collection of communications metadata and content as it passes through communications infrastructure
اعتراض صوتيّ	voice interception
اعتراض اتّصالات صوتيّة	interception of voice communications
تنصّت	wiretap
إلصاق جهاز مراقبة على هاتف	attaching a monitoring device to a telephone

7. ACRONYMS

تقرير بعد الحدث	AAR	after action report
استخبارات قائمة على النَّشاط	ABI	activity based intelligence
وكالة نزع السّلاح والحدّ من التّسلّح	ACDA	Arms Control and Disarmament Agency
أربع عيون	ACGU	Four Eyes
تحليل فرضيّات متنافسة	ACH	analysis of competing hypotheses
استخبارات صوتيّة	ACINT	acoustic intelligence
قسم الهندسة في الجيش	ACOE	Army Corps of Engineers
قيادة الأطلسيّ	ACOM	Atlantic Command
مساعد رئيس هيئة الأركان للقيادة والتَّحكم والاتَّصالات والحواسيب والاستخبارات	ACS/C4I	Assistant Chief of Staff for Command, Control, Com-munications, Computers, and Intelligence

مساعد رئيس الأركان لشؤون الاستخبارات	ACSI	Assistant Chief of Staff for Intelligence
نظام معلومات الوصول والمغادرة	ADIS	arrival departure information system
شبكة مكافحة المخدّرات	ADNET	antidrug network
تشغيل البيانات آليّاً	ADP	automated data processing
قاعدة قوّات جوّيّة	AFB	air force base
قيادة الاستخبارات الجوّيّة	AFIC	Air Force Intelligence Command
نظام التَّعرّف الآليّ على بصمات الأصابع	AFIS	automated fingerprint identification system
وكالة القوّات الجوّيّة للاستخبارات والمراقبة والاستطلاع	AFISR	Air Force Intelligence, Surveillance, and Reconnaissance Agency
وكالة الاستخبارات الجوّيّة	AIA	Air Intelligence Agency
نظام إلكترونيّ للمعلومات	AIS	automated information system

قيادة موادّ الجيش	AMC	Army Material Command
منطقة العمليّات \ موقع العمليّات	AO	area of operations
مجال اهتمام	AOI	area of interest
نطاق المسؤوليّة	AOR	area of responsibility
تهديد مستمرّ متقدّم	APT	advanced persistent threat
تقرير إداريّ	AR	administrative report
مساعد وزير الدّفاع	ASD	Assistant Secretary of Defense
مساعد وزير الدّفاع لشؤون الدّفاع عن الوطن	ASD-HD	Assistant Secretary of Defense for Homeland Defense
مساعد وزير الدّفاع للقيادة والتّحكم والاتّصالات والاستخبارات	ASD/C3I	Assistant Secretary of Defense for Command, Control, Communications, and Intelligence

جهاز الاستخبارات السرّيّ الأستراليّ	ASIS	Australian Secret Intelligence Service
مكافحة الإرهاب	AT	antiterrorism
المجلس الاستشاريّ لمكافحة الإرهاب	ATAC	Antiterrorism Advisory Council
تبادل معلومات لمكافحة الإرهاب	ATIX	Antiterrorism Information Exchange
نظام آليّ للاستهداف	ATS	automated targeting system
قانون أمن الطَيران والنَقل	ATSA	Aviation and Transportation Security Act
قوَة مكافحة الإرهاب	ATTF	Antiterrorism Task Force
مكتب الكحول والتَبغ والأسلحة النَاريّة والمتفجَرات	BATFE	Bureau of Alcohol, Tobacco, Firearms and Explosives
نظام تتبَع القنابل الحارقة	BATS	Bomb Arson Tracking System
مكتب خدمات المواطنة والهجرة	BCIS	Bureau of Citizenship and Immigration Services

تقدير أضرار المعركة	BDA	battle damage assessment
برنامج أبحاث الدَفاع البيولوجيَّ	BDRP	Biological Defense Research Program
استخبارات قائمة على القياسات الحيويَّة	BEI	biometrics-enabled intelligence
فريق الاستجابة لطوارئ الإرهاب البيولوجيّ	BERT	Bioterrorism Emergency Response Team
قائمة المراقبة المزوَدة بالقياسات الحيويَّة	BEWL	Biometrics-Enabled Watch List
تحقيق في خلفيَّة شخص أو منظَّمة	BI	background investigation
مكتب الهجرة والجمارك	BICE	Bureau of Immigration and Customs Enforcement
المهمَ في المقدَّمة	BLUF	bottom line up front
مجلس التَّقديرات الوطنيَّة	BNE	Board of National Estimates
إرهاب بيولوجيَّ	BT	bioterrorism

حرب بيولوجيّة	BW	biological warfare
شراكة جمركيّة تجاريّة ضدّ الإرهاب	C-TPAT	Customs–Trade Partnership against Terrorism
القيادة والسّيطرة	C2	command and control
حرب القيادة والسّيطرة	C2W	command and control warfare
القيادة والاتّصالات والتّحكّم	C3	command, communications and control
القيادة والاتّصالات والتّحكّم والاستخبارات	C3I	command, communications, control and intelligence
شؤون مدنيّة	CA	civil affairs
مركز العمل للأزمات	CAC	crisis action center
استجابة ومساعدة عند الحوادث الكيميائيّة	CAIRA	chemical accident or incident response and assistance
دوريّة الجوّ المدنيّة	CAP	Civil Air Patrol

خطّة العمل التّصحيحيّة	CAP	corrective action plan
الأهميّة وسهولة الوصول والاسترداد والضّعف والتّأثير والقدرة على التّمييز	CARVER	criticality, accessibility, recuperability, vulnerability, effect and recognizability
فريق عمل الأزمة	CAT	crisis action team
مركز الحروب غير المتناسقة	CAW	Center for Asymmetric Warfare
قيادة الدّفاع الكيميائيّة البيولوجيّة	CBDCOM	Chemical Biological Defense Command
قوّة الاستجابة للحوادث الكيميائيّة والبيولوجيّة	CBIRF	Chemical and Biological Incident Response Force
منظّمة قائمة على المجتمع	CBO	community based organization
حماية الحدود والجمارك	CBP	Customs and Border Protection

كيميائيّ وبيولوجيّ وإشعاعيّ	CBR	chemical, biological, and radiological
كيميائيّ وبيولوجيّ وإشعاعيّ ونوويّ	CBRN	chemical, biological, radiological and nuclear
كيميائيّ وبيولوجيّ وإشعاعيّ ونوويّ وتفجيريّ	CBRNE	chemical, biological, radiological, nuclear and explosive
فريق الاستجابة السّريعة للحوادث البيولوجية والكيميائيّة	CBRRT	Chemical Biological Rapid Response Team
حرب كيميائيّة وبيولوجيّة	CBW	chemical and biological warfare
مقاول مصرّح له	CC	cleared contractor
التّمويه والغطاء والخداع	CCD	camouflage, cover and deception
مراكز السّيطرة على الأمراض والوقاية منها	CDC	Centers for Disease Control and Prevention

مقاول مصرّح له التَّعامل مع وزارة الدَّفاع	CDC	cleared defense contractor
مجموعة الاستجابة للكوارث	CDRG	Catastrophic Disaster Response Group
شبكة الإدارة الشّاملة للطَّوارئ	CEMNET	Comprehensive Emergency Management Network
قيادة مركزيّة	CENTCOM	Central Command
فريق الاستجابة لطوارئ المجتمع	CERT	Community Emergency Response Team
لجنة الاستخبارات الخارجيّة	CFI	Committee on Foreign Intelligence
استخبارات مضادّة	CI	counterintelligence
مكافحة التّجسّس في القرن الـحادي والعشرين	CI-21	counterintelligence for the twenty-first century
وكالة الاستخبارات المركزيّة	CIA	Central Intelligence Agency

مكتب تأمين البنية التّحتيّة الحيويّة	CIAO	Critical Infrastructure Assurance Office
مركز الاستخبارات المجمّعة	CIC	Combined Intelligence Center
مجموعة الاستخبارات المركزيّة	CIG	Central Intelligence Group
معلومات البنية التّحتيّة الحيويّة	CII	critical infrastructure information
مكتب الصّور المركزيّ	CIO	Central Imagery Office
رئيس قسم المعلومات	CIO	Chief Information Officer
حماية البنية التّحتيّة الحيويّة	CIP	critical infrastructure protection
قانون إجراءات المعلومات المصنّفة	CIPA	Classified Information Procedures Act
خدمات المواطنة والهجرة	CIS	Citizenship and Immigration Services

تقييم ضعف البنية التَّحتيّة الحيويّة	CIVA	critical infrastructure vulnerability assessment
مركز مراقبة الاستخبارات المجمَّعة	CIWC	Combined Intelligence Watch Center
رئيس هيئة الأركان المشتركة	CJCS	Chairman of the Joint Chiefs of Staff
فريق إدارة الأزمة	CMT	crisis management team
هجوم على شبكة حاسوب	CNA	computer network attack
دفاع شبكة الحاسوب	CND	computer network defense
استغلال شبكة الحاسوب	CNE	computer network exploitation
رئيس العمليَّات البحريَّة	CNO	Chief of Naval Operations
لجنة أنظمة الأمن القوميَ	CNSS	Committee for National Security Systems

الحاجة إلى المعرفة الخاضعة للسّيطرة	CNTK	controlled need-to-know
مسار العمل	COA	course of action
مركز الجاذبيّة	COG	center of gravity
استمراريّة الحكومة	COG	continuity of government
استخبارات مضادّة	COIN	counter-intelligence
استخبارات الاتّصالات	COMINT	communications intelligence
أمن الحاسوب	COMPUSEC	computer security
أمن الاتّصالات	COMSEC	communications security
مفهوم خطّة العمليّة	CONPLAN	concept of operation plan
الولايات المتّحدة القارّيّة	CONUS	Continental United States
صورة العمليّات المشتركة	COP	common operational picture
خدمات حفظ الأمن الموجّه لصالح المجتمع	COPS	Community Oriented Policing Services

رئيس المحطّة	COS	Chief of Station
تقرير موقع القيادة	CPR	command position report
استخبارات جنائيّة	CRIMINT	criminal intelligence
رسالة استخبارات مهمّة	CRITIC	critical intelligence message
استعراض قدرات وتقييم مخاطر	CRRA	capabilities review and risk assessment
برنامج تأهيل المخزونات الكيميائيّة لحالات الطُوارئ	CSEPP	Chemical Stockpile Emergency Preparedness Program
مركز دراسات الاستخبارات	CSI	Center for the Study of Intelligence
جهاز الأمن المركزيّ	CSS	Central Security Service
فريق الدَعم المدنيّ	CST	Civil Support Team
مركز التَحليل التَتبّعيّ والاستجابة للأمن الحاسوبيّ	CSTARC	Cyber Security Tracking Analysis and Response Center

مكافحة الإرهاب	CT	counterterrorism
مركز مكافحة الإرهاب	CTC	Counterterrorism Center
مكافحة التَّهديد الماليّ	CTF	counterthreat finance
الإنكار والخداع	D&D	denial and deception
نظام الإنذار الدَفاعي التِّلقائيّ	DAWS	defense automated warning system
مدير وكالة الاستخبارات المركزيّة	DCIA	Director of Central Intelligence Agency
مدير توجيه الاستخبارات المركزيّة	DCID	Director of Central Intelligence Directive
نائب رئيس الأركان لشؤون الاستخبارات	DCSINT	Deputy Chief of Staff for Intelligence
نائب مدير جهاز الاستخبارات	DDI	Deputy Director for Intelligence
نائب مدير العمليّات	DDO	Deputy Director for Operations

إدارة مكافحة المخدّرات	DEA	Drug Enforcement Administration
حالة الجهوزيّة الدّفاعيّة	DEFCON	defense readiness condition
إنذار مبكّر بعيد	DEW	distant early warning
تعيين الاتّجاه	DF	direction finding
نظام الإنذار العالميّ للدّفاع	DGWS	defense global warning system
وزارة الصّحة والخدمات البشريّة	DHHS	Department of Health and Human Services
وزارة الأمن الوطنيّ	DHS	Department of Homeland Security
مديريّة الاستخبارات	DI	Directorate of Intelligence
وكالة استخبارات الدّفاع	DIA	Defense Intelligence Agency
مركز التّحليل الاستخباراتيّ للدّفاع	DIAC	Defense Intelligence Analysis Center

البنية التّحتيّة لمعلومات الدّفاع	DII	defense information infrastructure
موجز الاستخبارات اليوميّ	DINSUM	daily intelligence summary
ضابط استخبارات الدّفاع	DIO	defense intelligence officer
مدير وكالة الأمن القوميّ	DIRNSA	Director of the National Security Agency
نظام الإنذار الاستخباراتيّ للدّفاع	DIWS	Defense Intelligence Warning System
مدير الاستخبارات الوطنيّة	DNI	Director of National Intelligence
مديريّة العمليّات	DO	Directorate of Operations
استغلال الوثيقة	DOCEX	document exploitation
وزارة الدّفاع	DoD	Department of Defense

نظام المعلومات الاستخباراتيّة لوزارة الدَفاع	DODIIS	Department of Defense Intelligence Information System
وزارة الطّاقة	DOE	Department of Energy
وزارة الدَاخليّة	DOI	Department of the Interior
وزارة العدل	DOJ	Department of Justice
وزارة الخارجيّة	DOS	Department of State
وزارة النَقل	DOT	Department of Transportation
مركز التَعافي من الكوارث	DRC	disaster recovery center
مديريّة العلوم والتَكنولوجيا	DS&T	Directorate of Science and Technology
إرهاب محليّ	DT	domestic terrorism
التَهرّب والهروب	E&E	evasion and escape
نظام إنذار الطّوارئ	EAS	emergency alert system

مقاتل ينتمي إلى صفوف العدوّ	EC	enemy combatant
مكافحة التّدابير الإلكترونيّة المضادّة	ECCM	electronic counter-counter-measures
تدابير إلكترونيّة مضادّة	ECM	electronic counter-measures
عناصر المعلومات الأساسيّة	EEI	essential elements of information
استنتاج المعلومات	EI	educing information
وباء جهاز الاستخبارات	EIS	Epidemic Intelligence Service
استخبارات إلكترونيّة	ELINT	electronic intelligence
أمن الإلكترونيّات	ELSEC	electronics security
مراقبة إلكترونيّة	ELSUR	electronic surveillance
كهرومغناطيسيّ	EM	electromagnetic
خدمات طبيّة لحالات الطّوارئ	EMS	emergency medical services

أمر تنفيذيّ	EO	executive order
مبنى المقرّ التّنفيذيّ	EOB	executive office building
مركز عمليّات الطّوارئ	EOC	emergency operations center
تخلّص من الذّخائر المتفجّرة	EOD	explosive ordnance disposal
وكالة حماية البيئة	EPA	Environmental Protection Agency
مستجيب الطّوارئ	ER	emergency responder
فريق الاستجابة للطّوارئ	ERT	emergency response team
أمن وضمان الطّاقة	ESA	energy security and assurance
تدابير دعم الحرب الإلكترونيّة	ESM	electronic warfare support measures
نظام المراقبة الإلكترونيّة للتّبليغ المبكّر عن الأوبئة القاعدة على المجتمع	ESSENCE	Electronic Surveillance System for the Early Notification of Community-Based Epidemics

اتّصالات في حالات الطّوارئ	ETC	emergency tele-communications
القيادة الأوروبيّة	EUCOM	European Command
حرب إلكترونيّة	EW	electronic warfare
إدارة الطّيران الاتّحاديّ	FAA	Federal Aviation Administration
مكتب التّحقيقات الفيديراليّ	FBI	Federal Bureau of Investigation
استخبارات أجنبيّة مضادّة	FCI	foreign counterintelligence
الوكالة الاتّحاديّة لإدارة الطّوارئ	FEMA	Federal Emergency Management Agency
معلومات حكومة أجنبيّة	FGI	foreign government information
موادّ استخباراتيّة جاهزة	FI	finished intelligence
استخبارات أجنبيّة	FI	foreign intelligence
دفاع داخليّ أجنبيّ	FID	foreign internal defense

كيان الاستخبارات الأجنبيّة	FIE	foreign intelligence entity
تقرير معلومات ميدانيَ	FIR	field information report
متطلّبات وفئات وأولويّات لاستخبارات أجنبيّة	FIRCAP	foreign intelligence requirements categories and priorities
قانون مراقبة الاستخبارات الأجنبيّة	FISA	Foreign Intelligence Surveillance Act
استخبارات إشارات الأجهزة الأجنبيّة	FISINT	foreign instrumental signals intelligence
دليل العمليّات الميدانيّة	FOG	field operations guide
قانون حرّيّة المعلومات	FOIA	Freedom of Information Act
استخبارات الموادَ الأجنبيّة	FORMAT	foreign material intelligence
للاستخدام الرَّسميّ فقط	FOUO	for official use only
بيانات محظورة مسبقاً	FRD	formerly restricted data

الخطّة الاتّحاديّة لمواجهة حالات الطّوارئ الإشعاعيّة	FRERP	Federal Radiological Emergency Response Plan
المركز الاتّحاديّ للتّقييم والرّصد الإشعاعيّ	FRMAC	Federal Radiological Monitoring and Assessment Center
الخطّة الاتّحاديّة للاستجابة	FRP	Federal Response Plan
الإدارة الاتّحاديّة للمرور	FTA	Federal Transit Administration
فرقة العمل لتتبّع الإرهابيّين الأجانب	FTTTF	Foreign Terrorist Tracking Task Force
خمس عيون	FVEY	Five Eyes
شبكة معلومات العدالة الجنائيّة العالميّة	GCJIN	Global Criminal Justice Information Network
معلومات عالميّة ونظام إنذار مبكّر	GIEWS	Global Information and Early Warning System

ورود معلومات غير مقصودة وعديمة المعنى، واستخلاص معلومات غير مقصودة وعديمة المعنى	GIGO	garbage in, garbage out
بنية تحتيّة عالميّة للمعلومات	GII	global information infrastructure
نظم المعلومات الجغرافيّة	GIS	geographic information systems
نظام عالميّ لتحديد المواقع	GPS	global positioning system
تحليل المخاطر ونقطة التحكّم المهمّة	HACCP	hazard analysis and critical control point
موادّ خطرة	HAZMAT	hazardous material
الدَفاع الوطنيّ	HD	homeland defense
النَظام الإنسانيّ للإنذار المبكّر	HEWS	humanitarian early warning system

الصّحّة والخدمات الإنسانيّة	HHS	health and human services
منطقة تهريب المخدّرات بكثافة عالية	HIDTA	high intensity drug trafficking area
منطقة حدوث الجرائم الماليّة بكثافة عالية	HIFCA	high intensity financial crime area
تحديد المخاطر وتقييم الضّعف	HIVA	hazard identification and vulnerability assessment
الأمن الوطنيّ	HLS	homeland security
وكالة مشاريع البحوث المتقدّمة للأمن الوطنيّ	HSARPA	Homeland Security Advanced Research Projects Agency
النّظام الاستشاريّ للأمن الوطنيّ	HSAS	Homeland Security Advisory System
مجلس الأمن الوطنيّ	HSC	Homeland Security Council

مركز عمليّات الأمن الوطنيّ	HSOC	Homeland Security Operations Center
توجيه رئاسيّ للأمن الوطنيّ	HSPD	Homeland Security Presidential Directive
استخبارات بشريّة	HUMINT	human intelligence
هدف عالي القيمة	HVT	high value target
مؤشّرات وتحذير	I&W	indications and warning
تحليل المعلومات	IA	information analysis
ضمان المعلومات	IA	information assurance
الوكالة الدَّوليّة للطّاقة الذَّريّة	IAEA	International Atomic Energy Agency
تحليل المعلومات وحماية البنية التَّحتيّة	IAIP	information analysis and infrastructure protection
خطّة إجراءات الحادث	IAP	incident action plan

مجتمع استخباراتيّ	IC	intelligence community
صواريخ بالستيّة عابرة للقارّات	ICBM	inter-continental ballistic missile
التّضليل بواسطة الاتّصالات المزيّفة	ICD	imitative communication deception
إدارة تطبيق قوانين الهجرة والجمارك	ICE	immigration and customs enforcement
جهاز تفجيريّ يدويّ الصّنع	IED	improvised explosive device
تحديد صديق أم عدوّ	IFF	identification friend or foe
تفسير الصّور	II	imagery interpretation
قائمة مؤشّرات	IL	indicator list
استخبارات التّصوير	IMINT	imagery intelligence
جهاز نوويّ يدويّ الصّنع	IND	improvised nuclear device
أمن المعلومات	INFOSEC	information security

نظام المعلومات	INFOSYS	information system
حرب المعلومات	INFOWAR	information warfare
مكتب الاستخبارات والأبحاث	INR	Bureau of Intelligence and Research
خدمة الهجرة والتَّجنيس	INS	Immigration and Naturalization Service
تقرير استخباراتيّ	INTREP	intelligence report
ملخَّص استخباراتيّ	INTSUM	intelligence summary
معلومات العمليّات	IO	information operations
مجلس مراقبة الاستخبارات	IOB	intelligence oversight board
حماية البنية التَّحتيّة	IP	infrastructure protection
استجابة للحوادث	IR	incident response
نظام معلومات للاستجابة للحوادث	IRIS	incident response information system

تفَوّق معلوماتيَ	IS	information superiority
استخبارات ومراقبة واستطلاع	ISR	intelligence, surveillance, and reconnaissance
إرهاب دوليَ	IT	international terrorism
فرقة العمل الاستخباراتيّة	ITF	intelligence task force
حرب المعلومات	IW	information warfare
مركز التَّحليل المشترك	JAC	Joint Analysis Center
هيئة الأركان المشتركة	JCS	Joint Chiefs of Staff
مركز الاستخبارات المشتركة	JIC	Joint Intelligence Center
مركز العمليّات المشتركة	JOC	Joint Operations Center
قيادة العمليّات الخاصّة المشتركة	JSOC	Joint Special Operations Command
فرقة العمل المشتركة	JTF	Joint Task Force
فرقة العمل المشتركة لمكافحة الإرهاب	JTTF	Joint Terrorism Task Force

فريق عامل مشترك لمكافحة الإرهاب	JTWG	Joint Terrorism Working Group
النّظام العالميّ المشترك للاتّصالات الاستخباراتيّة	JWICS	Joint Worldwide Intelligence Communication System
سؤال استخباراتيّ رئيسيّ	KIQ	key intelligence question
استخبارات ليزريّة	LASINT	laser intelligence
وكالة فرض القانون	LEA	law enforcement agency
ملحق قانونيّ	LEGAT	Legal Attaché
الوحدة الاستخباراتيّة لفرض القانون	LEIU	Law Enforcement Intelligence Unit
برنامج فرض قانون مكافحة الإرهاب	LETPP	Law Enforcement Terrorism Prevention Program
صراع منخفض الحدّة	LIC	low intensity conflict
نشر محدود	LIMDIS	limited dissemination
ضابط اتّصال	LNO	liaison officer
استخدام رسميّ محدود	LOU	limited official use

احتماليّة ضعيفة للكشف	LPD	low probability of detection
احتماليّة ضعيفة للاعتراض	LPI	low probability of intercept
استخبارات القياس والإشارات	MASINT	measurement and signals intelligence
تبادل المعلومات بين دول لمكافحة الإرهاب	MATRIX	Multistate Antiterrorism Information Exchange
فريق العمل العسكريّ-المدنيّ للاستجابة للطّوارئ	MCTFER	Military–Civilian Task Force for Emergency Response
استخبارات طبّيّة	MEDINT	medical intelligence
استخبارات عسكريّة	MI	Military Intelligence
جهاز الأمن الدّاخليّ البريطانيّ	MI5	British internal security service
الجهاز البريطانيّ للاستخبارات الخارجيّة	MI6	British foreign intelligence service
مجلس الاستخبارات العسكريّة	MIB	Military Intelligence Board

أسلوب العمل	MO	modus operandi
مذكَّرة الاتَّفاق	MOA	memorandum of agreement
مذكَّرة التَّفاهم	MOU	memorandum of understanding
الدَعم العسكريّ لسلطات مدنيّة	MSCA	military support to civil authorities
منظَّمة حلف شمال الأطلسيّ	NATO	North Atlantic Treaty Organization
نظام الإنذار الوطنيّ	NAWAS	National Warning System
مركز التَّحليل الوطنيّ لأسلحة الدَفاع الحيويَة	NBDAC	National Bio-Weapons Defense Analysis Center
المركز الوطنيّ للأمراض المعديّة	NCID	National Center For Infectious Disease
خطَّة الطَوارئ الوطنيّة	NCP	National Contingency Plan
الجهاز السَرّيّ الوطنيّ	NCS	National Clandestine Service

حسّاسة غير حيويّة	NCS	non-critical sensitive
مركز الأمن الحاسوبيّ الوطنيّ	NCSC	National Computer Security Center
المركز الوطنيّ لمكافحة الإرهاب	NCTC	National Counter-terrorism Center
النّظام الوطنيّ الطّبيّ للكوارث	NDMS	National Disaster Medical System
الخطّة الوطنيّة للإعادة إلى الوطن في حالة الطّوارئ	NERP	National Emergency Repatriation Plan
المركز الوطنيّ للتّقييم الخارجيّ	NFAC	National Foreign Assessment Center
المجلس الوطنيّ للاستخبارات الخارجيّة	NFIB	National Foreign Intelligence Board
المجتمع الوطنيّ للاستخبارات الخارجيّة	NFIC	National Foreign Intelligence Community
البرنامج الوطنيّ للاستخبارات الخارجيّة	NFIP	National Foreign Intelligence Program

الوكالة الوطنيّة للاستخبارات الجغرافيّة الفضائيّة	NGA	National Geospatial-Intelligence Agency
منظّمة غير حكوميّة	NGO	non-governmental organization
المركز الوطنيّ لتحديد المهامّ للمتطلّبات الاستخباراتيّة البشريّة	NHRTC	National HUMINT Requirements Tasking Center
هيئة الاستخبارات الوطنيّة	NIA	National Intelligence Authority
النّظام الوطنيّ للإبلاغ على أساس الحوادث	NIBRS	National Incident-Based Reporting System
المجلس الوطنيّ للاستخبارات	NIC	National Intelligence Council
المركز الوطنيّ للتّنسيق بين الوكالات	NICC	National Interagency Coordination Center
تقدير الاستخبارات الوطنيّة	NIE	National Intelligence Estimate

البنية التَّحتيّة للمعلومات الوطنيّة	NII	National Information Infrastructure
نظام إدارة الحوادث الوطنيّة بين الوكالات	NIIMS	National Interagency Incident Management System
ضابط الاستخبارات الوطنيَ	NIO	national intelligence officer
مركز حماية البنية التَّحتيّة الوطنيّة	NIPC	National Infrastructure Protection Center
فريق الاستجابة للحوادث النوويّة	NIRT	Nuclear Incident Response Team
مركز المهامّ للاستخبارات الوطنيّة	NITC	National Intelligence Tasking Center
فرقة العمل الوطنيّة المشتركة لمكافحة الإرهاب	NJTTF	National Joint Terrorism Task Force
غطاء غير رسميّ	NOC	non-official cover

ممنوع التَّوزيع الأجنبيَ	NOFORN	no foreign distribution
قوَة الدَفاع الجوَيَ لأمريكا الشَماليَّة	NORAD	North American Aerospace Defense Force
القيادة الشَماليّة	NORTHCOM	Northern Command
مركز المعلومات البحريَة لمراقبة المحيط	NOSIC	Naval Ocean Surveillance Information Center
مركز الحدَ من الانتشار	NPC	Non-Proliferation Center
لا شيء مسجَل ضدَ	NRA	nothing recorded against
اللَجنة التَنظيميَة الوطنيَة	NRC	national regulatory commission
مكتب الاستطلاع الوطنيَ	NRO	National Reconnaissance Office
خطَة الاستجابة الوطنيَة	NRP	National Response Plan
وكالة الأمن القوميَ	NSA	National Security Agency

مجلس الأمن القوميّ	NSC	National Security Council
توجيه الأمن القوميّ	NSD	National Security Directive
القوّة الضّاربة الوطنيّة	NSF	National Strike Force
معلومات الأمن القوميّ	NSI	national security information
مركز عمليّات الأمن القوميّ	NSOC	National Security Operations Center
مراجعة الأمن القوميّ	NSR	National Security Review
خطّة البحث والإنقاذ الوطنيّة	NSRP	National Search and Rescue Plan
حدث الأمن الوطنيّ الخاصّ	NSSE	national security special event
مركز تقييم التّهديد الوطنيّ	NTAC	National Threat Assessment Center
استخبارات نوويّة	NUCINT	nuclear intelligence

برنامج عدم الانتشار وأبحاث التّحقّق والتّنمية	NVRD	non-proliferation and verification research and development
ترتيب المعركة	OB	order of battle
مكتب التّأهّب المحلّيّ	ODP	Office of Domestic Preparedness
مكتب التّأهّب الطّارئ	OEP	Office of Emergency Preparedness
مكتب الاستجابة لحالات الطّوارئ	OER	Office of Emergency Response
مكتب خدمات الطّوارئ	OES	Office of Emergency Services
مكتب الأمن الوطنيّ	OHS	Office of Homeland Security
مركز التّنسيق الاستخباراتيّ التّشغيليّ	OICC	Operational Intelligence Coordination Center
مكتب الاستخبارات البحريّة	ONI	Office of Naval Intelligence

عمليّات غير حربيّة	OOTW	operations other than war
موقع مراقبة	OP	observation post
السّيطرة على العمليّات	OPCON	operational control
عمليّات	OPS	operations
أمن العمليّات	OPSEC	operational security
دليل العمليّات	OPSMAN	operations manual
استخبارات بصريّة	OPTINT	optical intelligence
مكتب وزير الدّفاع	OSD	Office of the Secretary of Defense
استخبارات المصادر المفتوحة	OSINT	open source intelligence
مكتب العمليّات الخاصّة	OSO	Office of Special Operations
مكتب الخدمات الاستراتيجيّة	OSS	Office of Strategic Services
عميل رئيسيّ	PA	principal agent
قيادة المحيط الهادي	PACOM	Pacific Command

معلومات محميّة عن البنية التّحتيّة الحيويّة	PCII	protected critical infrastructure information
الموجز اليوميّ للرّئيس	PDB	President's Daily Brief
توجيه القرار الرّئاسيّ	PDD	Presidential Decision Directive
المجلس الاستشاريّ للاستخبارات الخارجيّة الخاصّة بالرّئيس	PFIAB	President's Foreign Intelligence Advisory Board
استخبارات الصّورة	PHOTINT	photo intelligence
شركاء في الحماية	PIP	partners in protection
متطلّبات استخباراتيّة ذات أولويّة	PIR	priority intelligence requirements
شخصيّة غير مرغوب بها	PNG	persona non grata
نقطة الاتّصال \ نقطة الالتماس	POC	point of contact
عمليّات نفسيّة	PSYOP	psychological operations
عناصر تهديد محتملة	PTE	potential threat elements

قسم تقييم الخطر	RAD	Risk Assessment Division
استخبارات الرّادار	RADINT	radar intelligence
خطّة إقليميّة طارئة	RCP	Regional Contingency Plan
بيانات مقيّدة	RD	restricted data
المركز الإقليميّ للعمليّات الطّارئة	REOC	Regional Emergency Operations Center
فريق الاستجابة للطّوارئ الإشعاعيّة	RERT	Radiological Emergency Response Team
طلب معلومات	RFI	request for information
طلب معلومات استخباراتيّة	RII	request for intelligence information
حسّاس للمخاطرة	RS	risk sensitive
قوّة الاستجابة للمهامّ	RTF	response task force
العلوم والتّكنولوجيا	S&T	science and technology
عميل خاصّ مسؤول	SAC	special agent in charge

القيادة الجوّيّة الاستراتيجيّة	SAC	Strategic Air Command
شعبة الأنشطة الخاصّة	SAD	Special Activities Division
معلومات المصادر والأساليب	SAMI	sources and methods information
برنامج الوصول الخاصّ	SAP	Special Access Program
البحث والانقاذ	SAR	search and rescue
حسّاس لكن غير مصنّف	SBU	sensitive but unclassified
لجنة مجلس الشّيوخ لشؤون الاستخبارات	SCCI	Senate Select Committee on Intelligence
معلومات مقسّمة حسّاسة	SCI	sensitive compartmented information
مرفق المعلومات المقسّمة الحسّاسة	SCIF	sensitive compartmented information facility
وزير الدّفاع	SECDEF	Secretary of Defense
استخبارات خاصّة	SI	special intelligence

استخبارات الإشارات	SIGINT	signals intelligence
أمن الإشارات	SIGSEC	signals security
عمليّات المعلومات الخاصّة	SIO	special information operations
جهاز الاستخبارات السّرّيّ البريطانيّ	SIS	UK Secret Intelligence Service
تقرير عن الوضع الحاليّ	SITREP	situation report
خبير في مجال معيّن	SME	subject matter expert
تقدير الاستخبارات الوطنيّة الخاصّة	SNIE	Special National Intelligence Estimate
الحاجة الخاصّة إلى المعرفة	SNTK	special need-to-know
إجراءات التّشغيل القياسيّة	SOP	standard operating procedures
اتّصالات الاستخبارات الخاصّة	SPINT-COMM	special intelligence communication
ضابط الأمن الخاصّ	SSO	special security officer

الأسلحة والتّكتيكات الخاصّة	SWAT	special weapons and tactics
نقاط القوّة والضّعف والفرص والتّهديدات	SWOT	strengths, weaknesses, opportunities and threats
استخبارات تكتيكيّة	TACINTEL	tactical intelligence
تقييم التّهديد البيئيَ	TEA	threat environment assessment
حالة التّهديد	THREAT-CON	threat condition
استخبارات تقنيّة	TI	technical intelligence
ملحق حادث إرهابيَ	TIA	Terrorist Incident Annex
استخبارات تكتيكيّة وأنشطة ذات صلة	TIARA	tactical intelligence and related activities
برنامج تحريم الإرهاب	TIP	Terrorist Inter-diction Program
معلومات الإرهاب والأنظمة الوقائيّة	TIPS	terrorism information and preventive systems

أمن البَثّ	TRANSEC	transmission security
إدارة أمن النَّقل	TSA	Transportation Security Administration
مركز الكشف عن الإرهابيّين	TSC	Terrorist Screening Center
مركز تكامل التَّهديد الإرهابيّ	TTIC	Terrorist Threat Integration Center
القيادة الموحَّدة	UC	Unified Command
معلومات نوويّة مراقبة وغير مصنّفة	UCNI	unclassified controlled nuclear information
جيش الولايات المتَّحدة	USA	United States Army
القوة الجوّيّة الأمريكيّة	USAF	United States Air Force
حرس سواحل الولايات المتَّحدة	USCG	United States Coast Guard
وكيل وزارة الدَّفاع لشؤون الاستخبارات	USDI	Undersecretary of Defense for Intelligence
قوّات مشاة البحريّة الأمريكيّة	USMC	United States Marine Corps

بحريّة الولايات المتَّحدة	USN	United States Navy
خدمة الولايات المتَّحدة السرّيّة	USSS	United States Secret Service
مراقبة الحالة	WATCHCON	watch condition
غرفة عمليّات البيت الأبيض	WHSR	White House Situation Room
أسلحة الدّمار الشّامل	WMD	weapons of mass destruction
النّظام العالميّ للتّحكّم والقيادة العسكريّة	WWMCCS	Worldwide Military Command and Control System

SELECT BIBLIOGRAPHY

Burton, Bob, *Dictionary of Espionage and Intelligence* (New York, NY: Skyhorse Publishing, 2014).

Central Intelligence Agency, *Glossary and Acronyms* www.cia.gov/library/reports/general-reports-1/iraq_wmd_2004/glossary.html (last accessed September 2014).

Denning, Dorothy, *Information Warfare and Security* (Reading, MA: Addison-Wesley, 1999).

Godson, Roy, *Dirty Tricks or Trump Cards* (New Brunswick, NJ: Transaction Publishers, 2001).

Goldman, Jan, *Words of Intelligence: A Dictionary* (Lanham, MD: Scarecrow Press, 2006).

Goulden, Joseph C., *The Dictionary of Espionage: Spyspeak into English* (Mineola, NY: Dover Publications, 2012).

Herrington, Colonel Stuart A., ret., *Traitors Among Us* (Novato, CA: Presidio Press, 1999).

National Security Agency, *Information Assurance Research* www.nsa.gov (last accessed September 2014).

Office of the Chairman of the Joint Chiefs of Staff, *Joint Publication 3–22: Foreign Internal Defense* (Arlington, VA: 2010).

Reagan, Colonel Mark L. (ed.), *Counterintelligence Glossary – Terms & Definitions of Interest for DoD Counterintelligence Professionals* (Washington, DC:

Office of Counterintelligence (DXC), Defense CI and HUMINT Center, Defense Intelligence Agency, 2011).

Reagan, Colonel Mark L. (ed.) *Counterintelligence Glossary – Terms & Definitions of Interest for CI Professionals* (Washington, DC: Office of Counterintelligence (DXC), Defense CI and HUMINT Center, Defense Intelligence Agency, 2014).

Smith, W. Thomas Jr., *Encyclopedia of the Central Intelligence Agency* (New York, NY: Facts on File, 2003).

INDEX